W9-CXT-683

# PIN-UP

# PIN-UP

## The Tragedy of Betty Grable

by

SPERO PASTOS

G. P. PUTNAM'S SONS
New York

G. P. Putnam's Sons
*Publishers Since 1838*
200 Madison Avenue
New York, NY 10016


Published simultaneously in Canada by
General Publishing Co. Limited, Toronto

Designed by Anne Scatto/Levavi & Levavi
Typeset by Fisher Composition, Inc.

Library of Congress Cataloging-in-Publication Data

Pastos, Spero.
Pin-up: the tragedy of Betty Grable.

1. Grable, Betty, 1916–1973. 2. Moving-picture
actors and actresses—United States—Biography.
I. Title.
PN2287.G66P37 1986 791.43'028'0924 [B] 86-8098
ISBN 0-399-13189-2

Printed in the United States of America
1 2 3 4 5 6 7 8 9 10

*This book is dedicated to the memory of my loving parents, William and Gregoria Pastos.*

# ACKNOWLEDGMENTS

This biography of Betty Grable could not have been written without the generous cooperation of the many people I interviewed—especially her daughter, Jessie James Yahner, her late sister, Marjorie Grable Arnold, and her lifelong friends Betty Ritz Baez, Paula Stone, and Charles Price.

In particular I would like to thank Carol Burnett, Jerry Herman, the late Charles LeMaire, Frank Powolny, Max Showalter, Bill Smith, Bill Travilla, Robert Wagner, and the following group of Grable confidants: Mikey Levitt, Richard Allan, Bob Isoz, Leonard Scumaci, and the late Jeff Parker.

I would also like to thank the many people who in one way or another offered their support, giving me their time, listening to and answering for me the endless questions I set before them: Jane Ardmore, Dr. Gus Bakos, Esther Baum, the late Anne Baxter, Councilman Ernani Bernardi, Josephine Brown, Bill Carey, Subrena Collins, the late Buster Crabbe, Christopher Deam, the late Leif Erickson, Alice Faye, Ned and Helen

Freeman, the late George Jessel, Howard W. Koch, the late Patsy Kelly, Dr. Robert Kositchek, Charles Lunard, Muzzy Marcellino, Virginia McClarand, George Montgomery, Franklyn Moshier, Terry O'Flaherty, Bob Osborne, the late Harriet Parsons, Ross Perry, Johnnie Ray, Ed Roginski, the late Helen Rose, Steve Searcy, Morton Smithline, Tony Wasserman, Pat Williams, and Sonia Wolfson.

A very special note of appreciation to 20th Century–Fox and to the UCLA Film Department, who permitted me to screen every Betty Grable film in their 20th Century–Fox Film Collection; the Academy of Motion Picture Arts and Sciences Film Library; the New York City Public Library at Lincoln Center, with its Chamberlain and Lyman Brown Agency Collection, and to the Museum of Modern Art Film Library.

# PROLOGUE

The 44th Annual Academy Awards held in April 1972 was an especially memorable event. Sentimentality and wistful nostalgia prevailed as 2,900 of Hollywood's finest joined to pay tribute to Charlie Chaplin. On this night he made his first and last appearance before an Academy audience. But it was Betty Grable who generated the real excitement that night. The film community was eager to welcome Grable back after almost fifteen years of self-imposed exile. Although the superstar of the 1940s had been the all-time favorite World War II pin-up and had worked over thirty years in films, Betty Grable, like Chaplin, was doing her first turn at the Oscar ceremony.

Academy president Howard W. Koch, an old friend of Grable's from their days at 20th Century–Fox, had arranged a spectacular musical tribute sung by Oscar winner Joel Grey and featuring a Grable look-alike in an upswept coif, white satin shorts, and ankle-strap shoes. The Grable clone descended the staircase, evoking memories of legendary Grable musicals, and when she struck the hands-on-hips pin-up pose, the audience broke into cheers.

It was a good omen. In recent weeks Grable had grown increasingly nervous about her hasty acceptance to appear. Like Chaplin, she felt the Hollywood community had forgotten her. Only hours before, overcome with anxiety, she had threatened to cancel and return to her hotel suite at the Beverly Hilton and then to Las Vegas, her home.

Koch recalled: "I thought it was a good time for her to appear at the Awards. I don't know why. I guess it was what my 'vibes' had told me and also whatever it is that moves you as a producer. But I thought putting her together with Haymes would be great." Dick Haymes had been Grable's costar in some of her biggest Technicolor hits.

It was the early 1970s and in the aftermath of the Vietnam War, America was feeling nostalgic again. Grable, the rage of the wartime 1940s, was the logical choice to spark a moment of patriotism. No one could have known that this would also mark her last major appearance.

When Awards cohost Sammy Davis, Jr., introduced her, the applause was deafening. Grable appeared genuinely surprised by the stirring reception as she walked briskly to the center of the stage, clutching Dick Haymes's arm. Looking out at the audience, she beamed a smile and fought to hold back her tears. Davis, an admitted lifetime fan of Grable, seized the moment to offer his own personal tribute. He bowed deeply and kissed her hand, before stepping away.

Still blonde at fifty-five, the deeply tanned Grable looked stunning in her low-cut, long-sleeved, turquoise-blue crepe and sequined Ret Turner gown that teasingly exposed the "million-dollar" gams. But after the first few moments it was clear to all that the famous pin-up image of thirty years before was forever gone.

In one of the most reproduced photographs in history, Betty Grable stood a slender young blonde in a white bathing suit and baby-doll pumps, back to the camera, peering over her shoulder with an expression of saucy innocence. The photo had been disseminated to countless millions of GIs in World War II.

Tonight Grable was stout and worn, the dimpled peaches-and-cream complexion dry and leathery from years of sun worship in the parched Nevada desert. Despite her makeup and blond wig, she looked puffy and her jowls sagged. It was as if she had finally become the tough, wisecracking, broadsy, heart-of-gold heroine she portrayed so well on screen.

As the applause died down, she nervously cleared her throat, leaned into the microphone, and speaking with an unfamiliar huskiness, read the list of nominees for the best original film score of 1971. The winner, Michel Legrand, the elegant French-born composer of the score for *Summer of '42,* made it clear he too regarded Betty as a legend by bowing and kissing her hand.

With his special tributes to Grable and Chaplin, Oscars producer Koch managed to resurrect the magic of Old Hollywood, as reflected in the Academy's list of most popular films—the sentimental favorites *Summer of '42* and *The Last Picture Show,* seemed to second him. The tribute to expatriate Chaplin, a gesture of forgiveness, was reflected by the Academy later that same evening when they awarded the Oscar for Best Actress to antiwar activist Jane Fonda for her splendid performance in *Klute.* Although Koch's tribute to Grable established her as the symbol of the grand Hollywood Technicolor musical, no honorary Oscar was forthcoming that night for Betty, underscoring the Academy's curious history of withholding the industry's ultimate accolade from its musical icons.

At the post-Awards dinner party at the Beverly Hills Hotel, friends made their way through the crowd to her table, eager to invite her to their homes during this rare Hollywood visit. But Grable politely declined them all, explaining she was about to depart for Australia to star in *No, No, Nanette.*

Her three traveling companions—lover Bob Remick, fan Mikey Levitt, and hairdresser Bob Latin—were well aware of the real reason she was eager to clear out of town: she was uncomfortable in the Hollywood social scramble and viewed it cynically. Grable felt the industry had abused her, and her years of protracted decline in movies had left a bitter memory. In 1957, when she'd left Hollywood for Las Vegas, Betty Grable swore never to return. Besides, she was addicted to gambling and dreaded any absence from her beloved casinos. And she was obsessively attached to two dogs who had become the great loves of her middle years—Kato, a Tibetan terrier, and Elsa, a German shepherd stray she had found wandering in a Vegas supermarket.

The morning after, Grable and her all-male coterie boarded the plane for the hour-long flight to Las Vegas. Jabbing her cigarette holder in her mouth and sipping her second martini of the morning, Betty suddenly let out a gasping moan. Then, in obvious pain, she clutched at her chest. The spasm passed, and she wondered aloud about the cause. Ordering another round of drinks, Grable and the boys decided it was nothing more than a psychosomatic symptom of Betty's fear of flying.

In Vegas, as they waited to collect their luggage, she doubled over again. This time the pain did not pass. Grable hissed, *"Something's wrong."* She was unable to walk or even to stand, so they carried her to an inactive luggage conveyor nearby, where she stretched out until the pain ceased. Her friends urged her to call a doctor, but Grable sat up and demanded a cab for the ride home. En route she insisted they stop at a local jeweler's to have her wedding ring from Harry James cut off her finger, disposing of a long-overdue chore. Gazing out the taxi's window as it sped across the desert—her home for the last fifteen years—Betty Grable sat uncharacteristically silent as the others in the party chattered on about the glitzy Hollywood weekend.

Once home, not even the lively reception of her beloved Kato and Elsa could overcome Betty's growing sense of foreboding.

# CHAPTER 1

. . . Daughters who have tried to live out their mothers' dreams end up with a diminished self. Little is ever felt—success, beauty, marriage, and wealth—because the daughter has always been her mother's extension and not her own person.

—Nancy Friday
*My Mother, My Self*

Betty Grable's mother was determined to make her daughter a star. Lillian Rose Hoffman, born May 29, 1889, in St. Louis, Missouri, was true to her astrological sign of Gemini—stubborn and materialistic, a social schizophrenic always in a constant state of flux. Her Quaker parents viewed her late arrival as a blessing and indulged her every whim. A beautiful, irresistible child, petite and frail-looking, Lillian had a flawless complexion and a finely chiseled porcelainlike face. Restless and headstrong, she tired of the stern religious practices and lectures her parents imposed on her and dreamed of escaping her stuffy existence to become an opera singer or actress.

"Her voice," Lillian's mother said, "was small, though very sweet-sounding—like the ring of crystal."

In the spring of 1904, at age fifteen, Lillian's career plans collapsed. Attending the centennial celebration of the Louisiana Purchase, better known as the St. Louis World's Fair, she met and fell in love with a ticket-taker. Conn Grable, stocky and strong, spoke in a hesitant deep baritone. With his fleshy cheeks, pug nose, bulging brown eyes, and bushy eyebrows, he looked like a bulldog. But Conn's was a gentle and loving nature. On their first chaperoned date, the two agreed to exchange nicknames—"Billie" and "Bud." Three years after meeting at the Fair, Billie and Bud married. He was twenty-one and Billie still a teenager. Free from the clutches of her overzealous parents, Billie willingly put aside her ambitions and plunged into homemaking, winning the approval of Bud's large family.

Before long, the honeymoon turned into a nightmare. Billie realized that the freedom she sought by escaping her family was not to be. She had landed in a Victorian milieu governed by strict mores. Bud tried in vain to draw Billie out of her depression. She did not share Bud's pride in his rapid rise in the commodities business, accomplished without the aid of formal education. And she bitterly denounced him for his devotion to his family, which she found smothering. Perhaps because of the tensions she was subjecting herself to, Billie developed a persistent and painful swelling in her hip.

Neither the social prominence Bud brought them as leading organizer of the first public utilities corporation in St. Louis, nor even the birth of their first child, Marjorie, could dissuade Billie from the conviction she had made a terrible mistake in marrying Bud. In her unhappiness she felt nothing but contempt for her daughter. A second child, a son called "Brother," died when the family physician, refusing to brave the late winter snows one night, crudely advised Conn to "just stick your finger down your son's throat and pull out the phlegm." By morning the twenty-month-old infant had suffocated, a victim of bronchial pneumonia.

Marjorie, then seven, witnessed her parents' bitter quarrel on the night of Brother's funeral. For the first time she remembered, she had sensed that the family was about to break up.

Billie was again pregnant when her mysterious hip ailment recurred. Her doctor prescribed an unorthodox and uncertain treatment, wrapping the swollen and inflamed hip in a leather casing punctured with hundreds of air holes. Doctors at that time disdained corrective surgery during pregnancy, fearing anesthesia would damage the fetus. Consequently, Billie lay confined to bed for the entire term.

It was during this period that she first developed a passion for the newest craze to hit America—tabloid scandal sheets and magazines full of Hollywood gossip. Immersed in escapist fantasies of movie glamour, her restless spirit at last found a home—somehow, Billie Grable swore, she'd get to Hollywood.

Elizabeth Ruth Grable was born on December 18, 1916. Shortly afterward, Billie discovered that because of extreme calcification, her hip had failed to set properly. She would be permanently disfigured. As Betty grew into a beauty, Billie's leg gradually deteriorated. The mother would find vicarious fulfillment in exploiting her daughter's legs and sexuality.

Throughout her life Betty Grable sustained a guilty sense of responsibility for her mother's injury. Billie often said she had fallen during pregnancy—and had made "the supreme sacrifice" for Betty. Marjorie, however, who never overcame her mother's rejection, claimed this was a fabrication her mother used to maintain close control over Betty.

During her big bid for Hollywood stardom, if Betty Grable ever displayed the slightest reluctance during her daily dance and musical workouts, Billie grabbed her by the shoulders and said, very slowly, "Betty, now you *know* why I walk the way I do. I sacrificed for you—now it's your turn to sacrifice for me."

It would never occur to Betty that Billie Grable had exploited her to satisfy her own frustrated ambitions. "It wasn't that mother ever pushed me," Betty said. "I was just simply raised to obey, no matter what it was."

Gertrude Temple, mother of another famous child star, once described how she manipulated her daughter, Shirley. "I wanted her to be artistic. I was determined she should excel at something: when I speak—she minds. There is no argument, no pleading and never any begging. I have also taught her not to be afraid of anything. I began the training very early and it meant vigilance. I soon learned not to let my affections make me too lenient."

Like Billie Grable, Gertrude Temple was a disappointed woman, never living her dream of becoming a ballet dancer. In 1974, when Gertrude lost the use of her legs in an automobile accident, Shirley Temple refused the advice of doctors urging amputation. For the last three years of her life, Gertrude, who died January 1, 1977, endured incredible pain to avoid the loss of her "ballet legs."

It was Hedda Hopper who would deliver the most damning judgment on stage mothers: "I used to wonder if there wasn't a sub-human species of womankind that bred children for the sole purpose of dragging them to Hollywood."

# CHAPTER 2

In 1922 golden-haired Betty Grable moved with her family from their comfortable home at 3858 Lafayette Street to St. Louis's fashionable Forest Park Hotel, where Bud rented an apartment suite complete with maid and room service. Billie enjoyed the hotel dining room, where she began mixing with visiting theatrical performers who appeared at the local Odeon Theatre, a major showcase in the vaudeville circuit. She often cornered these performers in the hotel corridors and instructed Betty to perform her newest song-and-dance routines. These embarrassing displays stuck in Betty's memory as among the most painful experiences of her childhood.

Billie knew from the tabloids that it was their mothers who had pushed teenage stars such as Mary Pickford and Lillian and Dorothy Gish. She was equally aware the mothers earned huge sums of money for their mysterious "services." Marjorie bore a strong resemblance to Bud, and Billie regarded this stubborn child as a poor candidate for show business. Betty, however, even at six, was beautiful. With her curly blond hair and alabaster skin, she was blessed with a bright smile revealing a perfect set of white teeth. All she needed, Billie believed, was musical training and luck. By her seventh year Betty had studied saxophone, piano, trap drums, ballet and toe dancing, tap dancing, and acrobatic dancing.

Billie's persistence paid off when Betty won a small dancing part in a kiddie show at the Odeon. From then on, Betty appeared regularly in the Odeon's annual Christmas shows featuring performers like comedian Frank Fay, who later married Barbara Stanwyck, and Jack Haley, the Tin Man in *The Wizard of Oz*.

Not surprisingly, the child's attendance at the fashionable Mary Institute, an exclusive girls' school, was remarkably sporadic, but Billie comforted herself with dreams of a major film career for her daughter. There is no evidence that Betty Grable ever finished high school. Marjorie Grable surmises that Betty never went beyond the seventh grade. The issue is further complicated by Billie's history of skillfully falsifying records, even legal documents.

In the summer of 1928 Billie persuaded Bud to drive the family to Hollywood for their vacation. She immediately enrolled Betty in a summer dance school and set out to explore the film studios. She was now even more determined to return to Hollywood with Betty—but with or *without* Bud.

The only remaining obstacle to Billie's dream was her daughter's growing self-assertiveness and independence, which Billie attempted to circumvent by promising Betty anything she desired in return for a deeper commitment to music lessons. Betty had developed a great passion for horseback riding in Forest Park; Billie shrewdly capitalized on that to guarantee Betty's full cooperation. If she applied herself to her musical studies, Billie promised, Betty could one day have her own horse. Now motivated, the girl plunged herself into daily lessons and rehearsals with renewed dedication, allowing Saturday-morning riding lessons as her only breaks. During this same period, Betty started a collection of porcelain and glass horses and filled her scrapbook to overflowing with photos and newspaper clippings about horses. Though she worked hard and waited patiently for the promised horse, it never arrived. "Daddy bought me a saddle once," Betty recalled, "but the horse never came. A saddle was useless without a horse. So I made them take it back and I was given a saxophone instead."

Betty's curious act of silent submission, when she had fervently prayed and longed for that horse for so long, is an early sign of the most self-destructive flaw in her character. Rather than face open confrontation with a detractor, Betty Grable waited behind a mask of stony-faced silence. When her antagonist was out of earshot, she would unleash torrents of venomous anger on any underling unfortunate enough to be at hand.

Because of the unpredictable state of the economy in the late 1920s, Bud's commodities exchange business was experiencing great difficulties. When he expressed grave concern for the family's financial security, Billie took Betty to California for the length of one school semester to explore the possibilities of a Hollywood film career for her. Billie and Betty headed west months before the crash of '29.

"Marjorie," Bud told his grieving daughter as they returned home from the train station that morning in January of 1929, "your mother does not know how to love anybody. I don't think she really loves Betty. She's just a piece of property."

Marjorie Grable Arnold would speak sorrowfully years later about her mother's departure, which left her behind along with her broken-hearted father: "I get more bitter as the years go by in that respect—I just didn't realize it at the time. She didn't give my father any of things that he wanted in a marriage, things that he deserved. All she wanted was help from him. Take—don't give. And she didn't just leave Conn. She walked out on me too. She was stagestruck, for cryin' out loud—absolutely stagestruck."

At thirteen, Betty Grable responded to a 20th Century–Fox casting call for beautiful showgirls, promising a film contract for the twenty winners. Attempting to sign up on the list along with hundreds of other hopefuls, Betty was asked to produce sufficient identification to verify her birthdate. Undaunted, Billie quickly altered Betty's hairdo, piled on more makeup, and pushed her through the front gate. She urged Betty to break into line and stand next to the shorter girls as a ploy to disguise her status as a minor. The ruse worked. Betty Grable landed her first film contract.

Director H. Bruce Humberstone was present that day. "There was no Central Casting at that time," he recalled. "I ran an ad in the paper for showgirls to come to the studio gate. Five hundred came and I picked out a few. They had to be sensational. The face was the thing. They didn't have to dance or anything—they just posed."

"It was like playing poker when you're holding four aces," Billie boasted. "I knew Betty had what they wanted."

In her first screen appearance in the quickie *Let's Go Places*, she danced in the chorus, made up in blackface. Later that year she served as a standby double for Mary Pickford in *Kiki*. At the same time, Betty attended Le Conte Junior High School, rather desultorily. Billie transferred her suddenly to Lawlor's Professional School for Children, then an unaccredited school, dismissing the warnings of her neighbors on Hollywood's Alexandria Street. Billie huffed, "It doesn't matter. Betty's going to be a star. What the hell's she gonna do with a college education?" Whatever the merits of Lawlor's $25-a-month educational program, it provided, at least, a social center for ambitious show-business mothers who attended the school regularly with their children. There they kept abreast of daily casting calls and auditions and exchanged gossip about the studio community. Mickey Rooney, Judy Garland, Jane Withers, and Gower Champion were among the hundreds of talented youngsters who attended the school with their mothers.

Had Billie not falsified her age, Betty could have attended the studio-maintained school for professional children working on the lot. Betty's contract listed her age as sixteen—the minimum age for working in the chorus, but overage for attending the studio school. Soon enough 20th Century–Fox discovered the discrepancy. All the major studios were now being closely scrutinized by federal and state labor agencies for violations of child labor laws, and a routine search uncovered the truth about Betty's age. She was immediately fired.

"That year with Fox wasn't altogether wasted," Betty said. "I had learned a lot about movies and what made them move. I knew that experience would be mighty helpful but the immediate problem, naturally, was how?" Billie proceeded to drag Betty all over southern California for appearances at benefits, hotel parties, and amateur-night contests.

Producer Harriet Parsons, daughter of Louella Parsons, remembered seeing Betty at a "mixed" bar at Christie's Hotel in downtown Los Angeles, where Betty was the featured dancer with the male singing-and-dancing team, the Rocky Twins. Parsons recalled that Betty had developed her first teenage crush on one of the twins. The fact that he was gay did not dissuade Betty from "leaning heavily on him." Throughout the rest of her life, Betty's closest friends would always be the male dancers in the chorus of her shows; she made them her confidants.

In 1930, along with Lucille Ball, Ann Dvorak, Anita Louise, Virginia Bruce, and Paulette Goddard, Betty was one of twenty-two girls chosen to become the original Goldwyn Girls. Struck by the success of Broadway impresario Florenz Ziegfeld's Ziegfeld Girls, Goldwyn decided he should have his own chorus line, but it wasn't until 1932, in *The Kid From Spain*, that he actually tagged them the Goldwyn Girls. Goldwyn spotted Betty's sexy legs and featured her in a production number in *Whoopee!* starring Eddie Cantor and coproduced by Ziegfeld.

During the first day of rehearsals on the huge soundstage, Betty danced down a steep flight of stairs, slipped, and fell. Embarrassed, she began to cry, looking to her mother for reassurance. "Do it again," Billie hissed, pointing to the top of the stairs. Betty slipped a second time, but now she retreated to the farthest corner of the stage, away from her mother. Billie stormed over and ordered, "Go back and do it again."

"No," Betty said. Taking Betty by the shoulders, Billie waited until Betty's eyes locked into hers. "Now look at me and listen very, very carefully. You will go *back* and you will start *again*. Now—go back." On the third attempt Betty pulled herself together. She was never to slip again.

*Whoopee!* was Betty's first featured role. In the opening

number, wearing what appeared to be little more than a G-string, a skimpy leather halter, a gun belt with two pistols, and a Stetson hat, Grable made her mark. Goldwyn was so impressed he used her again in his next three films.

*Palmy Days* featured her once more with Eddie Cantor and costarred the rubber-legged dancing lady, Charlotte Greenwood. Broadway actor George Raft played a hoodlum character named Joe the Frog. This was Raft's third film. When they met during shooting, Betty was fifteen. Raft, a fatherly thirty-six, had already established himself, among the Hollywood set, as something of a sexual stallion.

Raft was very attracted to Grable but feared she might reject him because of his age. He also worried about the Hollywood gossip columnists and what damage they might do to his career.

Betty was immediately attracted to the stockily built and deep-voiced Raft. Despite his sinister good looks, he reminded her very much of her father, whom she missed terribly. George managed to arrange for two chaperoned dates, but upon completion of *Palmy Days* he realized their relationship was notorious. Raft said, "I'm giving her back till she grows up."

In 1932 Betty was dressed in gowns by Chanel in *The Greeks Had a Word for Them.* Based on a Broadway play by Zoë Akins and starring Madge Evans, Ina Claire, and Joan Blondell, the story followed three beautiful gold-diggers in search of rich husbands. In succeeding decades Fox screenwriters would create several variations of the Akins theme, generously helping themselves to ideas from a similar play of that era, Stephen Powys's *Three Blind Mice,* originally filmed with Loretta Young, Binnie Barnes, and Marjorie Weaver. Grable was to star in two of the remakes, *Moon Over Miami* with Carole Landis and Cobina Wright, Jr., and *How to Marry a Millionaire* with Marilyn Monroe and Lauren Bacall. *Three Little Girls in Blue,* with June Haver, Vivian Blaine, and Vera-Ellen, was yet another gold-digger remake.

While Betty was still under contract to Goldwyn, Billie knowingly and illegally hustled her into eight two-reeler comedy shorts for RKO, Columbia, and the lesser-known Educational Films. Six of the eight were made for Educational and directed by Fatty Arbuckle, who used the alias William Goodrich. In 1921, at the peak of his career as a comedy star, Arbuckle had been accused of murder in the San Francisco bottle-rape death of actress Virginia Rappe. Billie was cautious in her dealings with Arbuckle and she demanded that Betty's name, in the film credits, be changed to Francis Dean. The Educational titles had a sleazy pornographic ring—"Crashing Hollywood," "Ex-Sweeties," "The Flirty Sleepwalker," "Hollywood Luck," "Love Detectives," and "Hollywood Lights."

In 1932, after Betty's fifth film with him, Goldwyn fired her without a word of explanation. Later, when she had established herself as a major star, Goldwyn recalled: "I had that girl under contract once. I wonder why I never did anything with her." Goldwyn, one of the most powerful producers in Hollywood, was probably aware of Betty's work with Arbuckle. As the self-appointed guardian of morality in films, he would have found the association highly improper. Nonetheless, years later, Goldwyn would approach Betty again.

# CHAPTER 3

Though it was the depth of the Depression in 1933, with box-office receipts having fallen from the 1929 record of $732 million to $482 million, and with employment down to an astonishing low, Betty Grable, now only sixteen, a veteran of eleven films, provided herself and her mother a luxurious existence. Billie had moved them into the fashionable Knickerbocker Hotel on Ivar Street in Hollywood where, ensconced in an apartment suite with room service, they remained comfortably insulated from the bitter realities of Depression America.

Billie gloated in her newfound freedom from Bud's nagging as she slipped Betty's earnings into her purse. Betty, realizing at last that her mother's promises to return home to Bud and Marjorie were yet another lie, began to explode in raging temper tantrums. But the more she rebelled, the more Billie saddled her with crushing workloads and hours of practice, auditions, and rehearsals. Billie even resorted to confining Betty whenever she disobeyed, locking her in the bedroom and, on more than one occasion, in the closet. Betty referred to these episodes as "jailings," pointing out that Billie left her locked up in the apartment while she visited friends for cocktails and poker. These repeated psychological abuses, this sadistic tampering with Betty's fragile emotional equilibrium left her with a disturbing and crusty hardening of her personality as she matured. Her waning will and broken spirit remained hopelessly fixated, burying forever the real Betty Grable. The slightest provocation now touched off raging outbursts in Betty. Family, friends, and work associates all fell regular victims to Betty Grable on the rampage; her tirades were poisonous in their intensity. Her life seemed set on a tragic parallel course with her ultimate screen image: the diamond in the rough—broadsy, explosive, short-tempered, tough, and independent. Cut off completely from her adoring father and older sister, Betty had developed a lonely and withdrawn personality. That her daughter was headed toward emotional suicide was ignored by Billie in her frantic pursuit of anyone who could help Betty's career. Curiously, not one of the many people who knew Betty at that time ever considered the tragic reality of her life. She was so highly exploited, immature, and totally lacking in self-confidence and esteem—a seemingly poor candidate for superstardom, and ripe to become its victim.

Restless and bored by the social formalities of the Knickerbocker, where she was unable to score professional contacts, Billie suddenly announced a move to the Canterbury, an apartment complex on the corner of Cherokee and Yucca in Hollywood, where a great number of actors, dancers, and vaudevillians lived.

In 1932 a major earthquake struck the Los Angeles area. Betty and her mother, along with other occupants of the Canterbury, including Dick Powell and Bert Wheeler of Wheeler & Woolsey, the comedy-film team, camped out together in a small park nearby until the tremors subsided. During the night Billie spoke with Wheeler at great length and shortly thereafter Wheeler cast Betty in his next RKO film, *Hold 'Em Jail,* a lowbrow comedy about a prison football game. An ingenue part was somehow written into the script for Betty. Billie's hunch to move to the Canterbury had paid off.

Billie now made her theatrical debut in the musical revue

*Tattle Tales,* starring Frank Fay and backed financially by Barbara Stanwyck. Opening at the Curran Theatre in San Francisco, the show was a hit and toured Santa Barbara and Los Angeles in preparation for Broadway. But Fay's drinking kept the company on constant edge and after a number of canceled performances, the show folded on the road, costing Stanwyck thousands of dollars.

Musician Muzzy Marcellino, together with his bandleader, Ted Fio Rito, caught the revue. Fio Rito described Betty as a "fantastic beauty" and felt she would be just right as the vocalist for the orchestra. "We didn't see very much of the show," Marcellino said, "for Fay appeared on stage in a drunken stupor and the curtain was quickly drawn." Fio Rito nevertheless hired Betty on the spot, along with Leif Erickson, who would later establish himself as a character actor.

Dance bands were the rage of the 1930s. Audiences crowded around the bandstands of great orchestra leaders like Paul Whiteman, Les Brown, Fred Waring, Ted Weems, Wayne King, Phil Harris, and Ted Fio Rito. The big bands played one-night stands at famous venues such as the New Yorker Hotel, Los Angeles's Coconut Grove and Ambassador Hotel, San Francisco's St. Francis Hotel, and Chicago's Palmer House.

A compulsive gambler, then only in his thirties, Fio Rito was a handsome man who would become a beloved father figure to a generation of young musicians and singers, many of whom went on to become stars. Fio Rito succeeded in creating a warm family feeling among the members of his orchestra, which included at various times Dick Powell, Wheeler & Woolsey, Leif Erickson, English-born musician-composer David Rose, who would later marry and divorce Martha Raye and Judy Garland; Bill Carey, who wrote the haunting ballad "You've Changed"; and Marcellino, who would later be the whistler on the hit recording, "Theme from *The High and the Mighty.*"

"You knew Grable was going to be something," Marcellino recalled. "You would look at her and say, 'I wonder what she looks like in the morning without the makeup.' She looked like a Dresden doll and had a figure that wouldn't quit. But a singer she was not."

For Grable those nine months with the band were to be

among the happiest of her life. From then on she would measure all her professional and personal relationships against the nurturing family she discovered in Fio Rito's orchestra. Too, it was generally recognized that musicians were considered the sex symbols of that era.

The spirit of camaraderie that existed among the family of musicians evoked in Betty a new and profound sense of belonging. And, insofar as her role models were musicians, she learned how important music was to them, how dedicated and disciplined they were. Grable decided to take her own responsibilities as a performer more seriously and to dedicate herself more completely to her career. But as the unofficial "pet" of the musical caravan, Grable failed to recognize one very important fact: the life of musicians on the road left some not-so-pleasant marks on the lives of their spouses and children.

Road musicians' wives—if they chose not to remain at home alone for months on end—spent their days in hotel rooms surrounded by total strangers. These women shared intimacies with hairdressers, bartenders, booking agents, hotel employees, and often, bookies. In time, as they tired of the road, the wives settled down to raise the children at home, waiting for their husbands to "drop in" after a series of lengthy tours.

Grable, who was not married at this time, failed to grasp these inherent problems. This flaw in judgment would leave her to face some very serious difficulties later in life, with tragic results.

Also with Fio Rito was a handsome young Kansas-born percussionist named Charles Price. Betty was immediately drawn to him and soon she and Charles were making plans for the nine-month tour that lay ahead of them.

Charles Price lives today in the Los Angeles suburb of Sherman Oaks. He recalls how Billie expressed her strong opposition to him by stipulating that he and Betty could date only when properly chaperoned. "Mrs. Grable didn't care too much about me. Betty and I would go to a movie, or a show, or dancing on a night off and Billie wanted us in by a certain time."

In a 1942 interview with Betty, gossip columnist Sidney Skolsky wrote about her first teenage dates. But instead of naming Charles Price, Betty mentioned George Raft. By the 1940s, Betty was again involved with Raft in a highly publicized romance. "She first met Raft," Skolsky wrote, "when she was working in the chorus of Frank Fay's revue *Tattle Tales.* She and her sister Marjorie, with her boyfriend, went out with him. 'I was just a squirt of fourteen or fifteen,' added Grable, 'and I had to be home by midnight.'"

Price was respectful toward Mrs. Grable, but after nine months of touring he knew she monitored Betty's every move—limiting the possibilities of courtship. Price remembers that Billie, despite her serious physical handicap, was a nice-looking woman with a warm smile who loved to laugh.

Marcellino vividly recalls how Billie exercised her extraordinary control over Betty when one night she herself chaperoned Betty on a double date with Marcellino and Price. "That woman was something else—a very strong-willed person. Charlie and Betty and this girl and I in Charlie's 'thirty-three Oldsmobile convertible went out on dates with Mrs. Grable chaperoning. But we made sure that Billie was anesthetized with wine."

The men put Billie in the rumble seat of the car as they sped toward San Francisco's foggy beaches. Then they stretched Betty's mother out on the backseat, where she fell asleep, unaware of the lovemaking taking place on the beach nearby.

During the tour a talent scout from RKO spotted Betty and signed her, but Betty refused to leave her young lover, tearfully begging Price to marry her and take her away with him.

"Betty, you can't go," Price said. "You can't leave, because you'd just create a lot of trouble. You've got a contract, and my God, you'd be stopped as a minor at the California border."

Betty stormed out of the room and Billie, realizing the seriousness of the attachment for the first time, also went into a rage.

Price says, "Betty was accustomed to living well. She wasn't ready to get married or fight off and sever all of those connections. I couldn't ask her to start living a married life in hotel rooms or a studio." Bill Carey states: "Charlie Price would probably have been a great guy for Betty. But it's funny the type of guys she finally married. Harry James always did exactly what *he* wanted."

"Charlie just couldn't keep me in silk stockings," Betty said. She had discovered wisecracks were the perfect way to take the edge off sensitive issues.

Both Bill Carey and Betty were sixteen-year-old minors, required by state law to continue their education, even while working on the road. Though Carey later earned his high school diploma, he could not recall ever having seen Betty Grable carry a book or do homework. "She must have attended *some* school," he added uncertainly.

It was Billie's disregard for and constant interruption of her daughter's education that reinforced Betty's deepest sense of inadequacy and inferiority. Throughout her life she would avoid social gatherings where she feared her lack of education might be exposed and subject her to ridicule.

# CHAPTER 4

In the early 1930s Betty Grable made films at RKO, Columbia, and MGM before attracting attention in a novelty song-and-dance number opposite Edward Everett Horton in *The Gay Divorcee*, which featured Fred Astaire and Ginger Rogers. Trade reviewers cited the "lilting" charm of the Mack Gordon–Harry Revel song "Let's Knock K-neez" and termed Betty's rendition "full of pep and very, very appealing." Edward Everett Horton said, "We all knew there was something special about her—something appealing that made you feel good inside."

In 1935 Betty was reunited with her old friends Wheeler & Woolsey in RKO's *The Nitwits* directed by George Stevens, a mystery-comedy in which Betty played the prime suspect in her boss's murder. Lucille Ball, in a bit part, appeared with Betty in *Old Man Rhythm*, in which they both portrayed coeds. Now at age eighteen, with twenty films to her credit, Betty took stock of her dubious accomplishments and decided there was no place for her in the movies. "I couldn't act any better," she admitted, "or dance any better than a dozen people I could name." At this point Betty Grable had worked for every major studio in Hollywood and not one of them knew what to do with her. With her low self-esteem it did not occur to Betty now, nor would it later, that she was the most dazzling beauty on the American screen.

In 1936 RKO promised that her appearance in *Follow the Fleet,* starring Astaire and Rogers and featuring music by Irving Berlin, would lead to major assignments, but her part was cut down to a few minutes in a backup trio of female singers for Ginger's "Pick Yourself Up." Betty resented the temperamental outbursts of the ambitious Ginger, who, with the support of her mother, Lela Rogers, asserted her star power by stepping on every chorus toe in sight. Betty never forgave Ginger Rogers. Later, when she far surpassed Rogers in popularity, the two women were icily cordial, barely tolerating each other.

Betty loaned herself out to Fox for the zany 1936 football musical comedy *Pigskin Parade,* but she was lost in a cast featuring Tony Martin, the brilliant comedy heavyweights Patsy Kelly and Jack Haley, and, in her screen debut, the diminutive fourteen-year-old singing wonder Judy Garland.

Although RKO had created the Grable peroxide style, promoting her as the "quicksilver blonde," studio executives decided to drop her from their roster of contract players after her disappointing performance in *Don't Turn 'Em Loose.* One producer described the reason for her termination: "She was cuter than most imitation coeds whipping around the lot, but her cuteness didn't seem to mean anything when she appeared. There were a few whistles but nothing to burst your eardrums. Although she was nicely stacked you could look at her all day without raising your temperature one degree."

Paramount used Grable for a "collegiate" film in 1936 and now they put her under contract, promoting her as the quintessential coed. The young actress posed on top of buildings, in the ocean, and even in a cage with a lion—invariably clad in the newly emerging skimpy bathing suit. Her spectacular legs had never been seen to such advantage. The pin-up craze was about to begin.

It was Bill Carey from the Fio Rito band days who introduced Betty Grable to Jackie Coogan. Carey was accompanying Betty and her mother on a cruise bound for Catalina Island when he bumped into Coogan and invited him to join their party. The four played cards until the boat docked, when they parted company.

A former child star, Coogan, who later went to the University of Southern California, was attending the University of Santa Clara, where he had become a cheerleader. He remarked to Betty that he often drove from Santa Clara to watch her weekend bandstand performances. Coogan had experienced great difficulty in his attempts to establish himself as a young leading man. As his career began to flounder he decided to enroll at Santa Clara, hoping a business major would prepare him to manage the multimillion-dollar estate built from his earnings as a major child star. Jackie was still recovering from the shock of his father's death, in an automobile accident he himself had survived.

In May of 1935 the senior Coogan had arranged for a special weekend celebration of his son's twenty-first birthday (which was actually not until late October) at the Coogans' Pine Valley ranch in San Diego County, a two-and-a-half-hour drive from Los Angeles. It was a late Sunday afternoon when Coogan, along with his father, juvenile actors Bob Horner and Junior Durkin, and the foreman of the Coogan ranch, headed back to join the others after a day spent bird hunting.

The large party had separated into three cars, with Jackie at the wheel of the brand-new automobile just given to him by his father.

One of the people who attended the celebration that day was radio actress and producer Paula Stone, who with a few others decided to remain at a nearby beach. She recalled: "Jackie drove like a madman—I mean he would drive so fast just to scare you. 'I won't drive with you, Jackie,' I said." Soon the state police drove up to Paula and her group and informed them there had been a terrible accident involving her friends. When they drove back to the scene of the wreck, Paula found bodies "scattered all over the place."

It was later reported that the elder Coogan, who died at the scene, had been the driver of the death car, but Paula Stone feels certain this was not so. "It has always been in the back of my mind, and though I never said anything because Jackie was a friend of mine, I was sure it was he who was driving." Bob Horner was decapitated and Junior Durkin, a popular screen actor, lay dying as Stone arrived at the scene. Jackie, ashen and clutching his arms to his broken ribs, wandered around the site, dazed and moaning in agony.

Five months later Jackie received another shock when the terms of his father's will were disclosed. Of the $4 million Jackie had earned as a child star, nothing had been left to him. Everything went to Jackie's mother, Lillian, with no provision for a trust fund for Jackie's future. The $4 million, Coogan's father had specified, would be reverted to his son only upon the death of his widow, Lillian Coogan. Lillian then married Jackie's business manager, Arthur Bernstein, and was named president of Jackie Coogan Productions, Inc. Bernstein, a former New Yorker, had a reputation among the studio powers as a shrewd investor. By helping Lillian gain full control of the Coogan estate, Bernstein made sure Jackie's fortune was no longer legally his, even if he should survive his mother.

Against this background of greed and exploitation, Betty Grable and Jackie Coogan met and fell passionately in love. Buster Crabbe, another Grable intimate, remembered how Betty and Jackie often went to the Santa Monica Social Club to cavort on the beach. They were in high spirits as they planned their future. Though the two golden blonds made for a physically stunning couple, there were deeper bonds drawing them together. Both were manipulated and victimized by their parents, who viewed them as profit-making properties and usurped their considerable earnings. Both yearned to be free from mothers coincidentally named Lillian.

The two Lillians disapproved of the proposed marriage. Billie managed to extract Betty's promise that she would not marry until her twenty-first birthday. On December 20, 1937, two days after her birthday, Betty married Jackie. As she left the church, she cried: "I want to be Mrs. Jackie Coogan for life!" Jackie, confident his marriage was off to a great start, boasted, "I'm soon going to receive a million dollars! I made it when I was a kid."

The formal church wedding, attended by 100 friends, made international headlines. Betty's sister, Marjorie, served as maid of honor while Bud Grable, though disapproving of Coogan, lovingly gave his daughter away.

Bud had never recovered his business losses after the crash. Now he was struggling with alcoholism. Still in love with Billie, he had faithfully continued commuting from St. Louis, hoping Billie would ask him to settle in Los Angeles. She did not; Bud felt he was an unwelcome visitor in *her* home. He too became financially dependent on Betty.

After the marriage, the young Coogans set up housekeeping in a rented house on Montana Street in Brentwood. On the first night after returning from their honeymoon, Betty, eager to cement relations with her family, invited her parents, Marjorie, and friends Paul and Virginia McLarand for dinner and an evening of cards. During the poker game, Bud, drinking heavily, grew hostile as he chided Jackie. Tension mounted when Jackie began to lose. Completely out of money, he offered to write a promissory note to Bud who, by then unable to restrain himself, thundered: "The hell with you—you has-been! If you haven't got the money then get your ass out of here!"

Even as a married woman, Betty's career continued to be manipulated by her mother. Dissatisfied with Paramount's handling of Betty for the last two years—she had appeared in seven films for them during this period—Billie stormed into the front office, ordering the studio to release Betty from her contract. Paramount refused on the grounds they had spent considerable promotional time and money in building Betty's career. Billie raised her cane and smacked the desks as she went into a screaming fit. She got the release.

Ugly rumors began appearing in the press, intimating Betty's primary interest in marrying "The Kid" was the money he would soon inherit from his childhood earnings. In reality, it was Betty who footed expenses for the wedding, honeymoon, automobile, and new apartment, including all the furnishings. She urged Jackie to sue his mother and stepfather for the inheritance that was rightly his. Thanks to her prodding, he finally filed a lawsuit against his mother. The press reported the scandal along with accounts of the newlyweds' frequent quarrels.

"I'm not really bitter at Jackie," Mama Bernstein told reporters, "I'm just filled with regret that I should have put so much time and spent so much money trying to make the right sort of man out of him only to discover that he really is very stupid."

Jackie was still smarting over the scandal his mother had precipitated in 1928, when the first Mrs. Arthur Bernstein—in a $750,000 alienation-of-affection suit—charged that Lillian Coogan, then still married to Jackie's father, had been "too friendly, for about two years," with her husband. Jackie never forgave his mother's transgression, especially later, when she married Bernstein. "My mother," Coogan told the press, "was influenced by Bernstein, and had my father still been living this suit would not have been necessary." When he announced his engagement to Betty, Lillian Bernstein, instead of offering her blessing, blasted back, "The 'Millionaire Kid' didn't have enough to take me dancing, let alone get married."

Billie recognized the potential financial rewards to be reaped now that Betty and Jackie were front-page news. She exploited the problems surrounding her daughter's difficult marital predicament by arranging to have Betty and Jackie appear together in a nationwide vaudeville tour.

The press began to turn sour on Betty. Gossip columnist Sheilah Graham viciously wrote: "The most overpublicized girl in the movies is saying goodbye to Hollywood—without having made the picture grade. I refer to Betty Grable, the youngster whose roles did not succeed in catching up with the oodles of publicity of which she was the heroine. She was pictured laying the cornerstone of this and that, photographed with every visitor to Paramount Studios, on hand for every convention in town, and all in all kept so busy that there was no possible time to make anything beyond a quickie college feature."

At the infamous Coogan trial, the court forced Bernstein to pay Jackie $126,307.50 as settlement for the squandered millions, but after expenses Coogan was left with only $35,000, which included money from life insurance. Clearly it was no victory for Jackie; and the trial had placed impossible strains on his marriage. "It was a living nightmare," Betty confided to her friend Betty Ritz. On January 20, 1939, Grable announced their separation; later they would be divorced. "Jackie suggested the separation," she admitted. "I didn't. Until we get things worked out. I'd go back to him in a minute—if he'd ask me."

Reporters asked if she was leaving Coogan because he didn't have any money. She replied: "Such silly talk. The lease expired on our house. I thought we ought to move to a smaller place or live with my mother. The first thing I knew Jackie was selling the furniture. Boom! And all my stuff moved out. Then he said he was going to San Francisco to see about an act. But he didn't ask me to go with him. I don't know why Jackie hasn't said anything to defend me. I still love him and he knows it. Maybe it was his lawyer's idea. He didn't talk very much . . .

"I used to tell him that it was terrible for him to stay in bed all morning. I thought he ought to get out early and at least look for some kind of job. I knew he didn't have any money when I married him. He's got more money now than he had then. It came from the sale of my furniture. I let him keep all of it . . .

"But here's the payoff. What do you think he did with some of the furniture money? He bought a new car! Can you tie that?

"I still love him and I'll go back to him whenever he asks me. But I won't chase him."

The real reasons for the breakup, Betty admitted later, were Jackie's drinking and flagrant infidelities. He had blatantly demonstrated his contempt for her by repeatedly bringing young starlets to their home, even when Grable was present. But always, Grable said, Coogan would apologize—and she "always, stupidly, forgave him." When she tired of his neurotic peccadillos and pleas for forgiveness, she departed on a tour of eastern cities with Eddie "Rochester" Anderson in an act that earned her $1,500 a week—incredible money during the Depression era.

Jackie Coogan would go on to four marriages, four children, and a series of drug and drunk-driving charges. Still, Betty Grable, when asked about her marriage to Coogan, would admit over a vodka and tonic in a bar years later, "Honey, Coogan taught me more tricks than a whore learns in a whorehouse!"

# CHAPTER 5

Never one to be upstaged by her daughter, on June 1, 1939, Billie announced to the press her divorce from Conn Grable after thirty-one years of marriage, charging mental and physical cruelty. She also added that Bud was living off Betty's earnings. With Betty appearing as a witness in court, Billie stated: "On May 28, 1938, the defendant [Bud] said he was going to leave to go back to his home in St. Louis as soon as he got his share of Betty's earnings."

Billie sought possession of their home at 250 Chadbourne Street in Brentwood, which Betty had paid for. Stating that she was under full-time care of a trained nurse because of a "nervous" illness caused by Bud's constant abuse and threats, Billie sought a restraining order to keep him from "molesting" her.

"From her bed last night," the *Los Angeles Herald Examiner* wrote, "Mrs. Grable said she was 'trying desperately' to regain her strength so she can accompany her daughter when the actress makes a personal appearance tour in a few weeks.

"'I've been with Betty every time she's gone on the road, and

I hope this [divorce suit] will clear things up so my nerves will settle down.'"

Singed by notoriety, Betty vowed she would never again allow the press to scrutinize her private life.

Betty had become romantically involved with Victor Mature. Now he followed her across the nation during her East Coast tour, cluttering her hotel rooms with "a fuzzy elephant, a teddy bear, and a doll with sleepy eyes." When the press besieged her with questions about Mature, she said their many dates really didn't mean a thing. "In the first place, I have an understanding with the studio that I'm not to be married again for at least another year, and in the second place, the man I marry hasn't come along yet."

Darryl F. Zanuck, the new production chief at 20th Century–Fox, had just signed Betty after spotting her in a publicity still, but he did not yet know what to do with her. When Jack Haley, Sr., wanted her for a two-week engagement at the San Francisco Exposition, Zanuck authorized her temporary release on condition she return to Fox as soon as he decided on a film for her.

In San Francisco, Louis Shurr, a New York theatrical agent, caught her song-and-dance routine and recommended her to producer-songwriter Buddy DeSylva, who was casting the new Cole Porter Broadway musical *Du Barry Was a Lady*. "But I've never been on the stage before," Betty said. "That's Broadway's loss," DeSylva murmured, hastily signing her for the ingenue role.

On October 11, 1939, a day before her departure for New York, she arrived in court for her divorce from Coogan on the arm of jazz clarinetist Artie Shaw. Hovering as usual, Billie smiled knowingly as reporters inquired about the possibility of a Grable–Shaw marriage. Betty said, "No comment," but Billie, seizing the limelight, prodded: "Why don't you tell the reporters, darling? It's nothing to be ashamed of, you know." Betty shook her head and began to push her way through the crowd.

Arriving in New York, again accompanied by Artie Shaw, Betty said, "We're very fond of each other, but I don't know about marrying him. My divorce doesn't become final until November 11, 1940."

In fact, Grable was absolutely mad about Shaw and they had already decided to marry, despite Billie's strong objections.

Many considered thirty-year-old Artie Shaw to be one of the greatest clarinetists in the world, rivaled only by Benny Goodman. Although Shaw's marriages to the screen's most celebrated beauties—Lana Turner, Ava Gardner, Evelyn Keyes—would come later, he had already developed a reputation as a virile lover and had been twice married and twice divorced. Recalling her first meeting with Shaw, Evelyn Keyes wrote: "Here was a presence. A strength I hungered for. Someone who could take me somewhere I had never been."

Before his romance with Betty Grable, Shaw had been involved with actress Lois Andrews, a former George White showgirl, and seventeen-year-old Judy Garland, who fell in love with Shaw just before making *The Wizard of Oz*. "You're little Frances Gumm from Grand Rapids and I'm Artie Arshawsky from the Lower East Side and now look where we are," he gloated to Judy. "We're the chosen few, Judy. We're the chosen people." More than ten years her senior, Shaw had teasingly encouraged young Judy to fall for him. Later he claimed he'd never thought of her as anything more than a "sister."

Shaw, a well-read intellectual, espoused the "will-to-power" theories of nineteenth-century German philosopher Friedrich Nietzsche. Restless, insatiable, and considered selfish and arrogant by many, he saw himself as a Nietzschean superman—with his dark good looks and sensual smile he charmed and seduced many of Hollywood's femmes fatales. In reality these young women were just pathetic lost souls battered by career pressures, ambitious and exploitative parents, worthless basket-case husbands, and ruthless studios. They came to him weary and vulnerable and ready for the answers he appeared to offer. "Near perfect," he assured them, they could attain perfection by serving him.

Shaw convinced Betty Grable that her career, though very promising, was incompatible with his concept of ideal marriage. Though Billie did not understand the subtleties of German philosophy, she knew enough to recognize an enemy when she saw one and began a systematic campaign to sabotage the relationship.

After a two-week tryout in Boston and another week in Philadelphia, *Du Barry Was a Lady* opened December 6, 1939, to good reviews on Broadway, a little over a week before Betty's twenty-third birthday. The stars of the show, Ethel Merman and Bert Lahr, received fine reviews, but it was Betty's performance that impressed and surprised the hard-boiled New York critics. "Miss Grable was not what I expected and feared," Sidney Whipple wrote in the *New York World Telegram*. "She was actually good, despite her Hollywood training." *Time* said: "She performs like a thoroughbred. Not so blonde as pictured, Miss Grable is a lovely little trick who knows her stuff in both songs and dances. Most of the hoofing is with Charles Walters and they make a scoring team . . . Probably it is the careful training as a kid that stands her in good stead now."

Walters sang and danced with Betty in the song "Well Did You Evah!" But it was Betty's showstopper, "Ev'ry Day a Holiday," that made her a Broadway star overnight. She awoke on the morning of December 11 to find herself on the cover of *Life* magazine. The wonderful action photo showed an exuberant Grable leaping in midair toward the camera, costumed in her Louis XV gown from the show. *Life* wrote, "Betty Grable, twenty-two, takes her first bow as a musical comedy actress. She sings a little, dances some, and is the best thing in the show."

With characteristic reserve Brooks Atkinson, dean of Broadway critics, wrote in *The New York Times*, "Betty Grable who is best known to us as a movie actress makes in this musical her legitimate stage debut. She is a clever dancer and can sing a song. She proves that she has something else besides a pretty face." Cole Porter quipped, "If the show accomplished nothing else, it once and for all made it unnecessary to identify Miss Grable as 'Jackie Coogan's ex.'"

As *Du Barry* settled in for a successful run, Billie threw her campaign against Artie Shaw into high gear. Her screams resounded from their eighth-floor suite at the Essex House one afternoon when Billie overheard Betty accepting an after-theater date with Shaw. Wretchedly torn between her lover and her mother, Betty weakened when Billie resorted to gasping for breath and clutching her chest, miming a heart attack. Betty promised to cancel her date with Shaw.

Artie Shaw assured Betty he still loved her but suggested, "Why don't you push your mother out of the hotel window?" Recalling that miserable night to her friend Betty Ritz, Betty admitted she had experienced a tremendous urge to kill Billie. Instead she began planning her escape; the next day she sent a letter to Shaw by special delivery.

> Darling, this is what I've been waiting for. I've just handed in my notice to the show *[Du Barry]*. Let's get married tomorrow!

There was no tomorrow for Betty and Artie. The headlines for February 9, 1940, read: ARTIE SHAW MARRIES LANA TURNER. They had eloped to Las Vegas.

"That son of a bitch!" Grable shouted on the phone to Phil Silvers in Los Angeles. "Who does he think he is, doing this to me?" In tears she slammed down the receiver. Comedian Phil Silvers, a close friend of Shaw's, was caught up in the uproar following the wedding announcement. A broken-hearted Judy Garland also called him that morning. Silvers tried to console her by offering to drive her to school. "How could he do this to me," Judy moaned. "How *could* he?"

Lana Turner and Artie Shaw had both declared publicly that they detested each other when they'd worked together in the film *The Dancing Co-Ed*. In less than a year their marriage would end as suddenly as it began.

With the press at her door, Betty could only say, "It must have come on him very sudden." On a matinee day, accompanied by a very close friend, Betty, in the privacy of a West Side Manhattan doctor's office, underwent her first abortion. Billie never learned of it.

Still embittered from her years as a Hollywood starlet, Betty told New York reporters, "Hollywood has a way of letting you down that is rather discouraging. I guess the only reason I'm in a Broadway show now is that the films didn't want me. It comes as something of a shock after you've worked in several studios and been publicized around the country for years suddenly to realize there are no available roles for you."

When her complaints reached Darryl Zanuck's ears, he summoned her back to Hollywood on June 3, 1940. She was to replace Fox's leading star Alice Faye in *Down Argentine Way*. Alice had undergone an appendectomy and had been forced to cancel. The production could have been delayed a week, of course, to accommodate Miss Faye, but according to some observers, she had grown tired of her crown as "Queen of the 20th Century–Fox Musicals" and was eager to depart the throne and retire.

Upon Grable's triumphant return to Hollywood, Harriet Parsons was struck by the change in the once-naive starlet she'd first met in 1931, when Grable had appeared at Christie's Hotel with the Rocky Twins. Parsons said, "The youngster who left Hollywood with a failure complex has come back with all the assurance of a headliner."

# CHAPTER 6

Shortly after beginning an affair with Tyrone Power, Betty noticed a peculiar and persistently foul feminine odor. Mystified, she visited her physician but his examination of her yielded nothing.

She and Tyrone were costarring in the romantic drama *A Yank in the R.A.F.* that Darryl Zanuck had himself written, under the pseudonym Melville Crossman. Zanuck had just starred Grable in the musical *Moon Over Miami*—the first of three films she made in 1941 for Fox—and he was quite pleased with his photogenic creation. She was delectable in Technicolor with her shoulder-length dark brown hair. Later Grable would switch back to the blond hair that would become a trademark. The industry was shocked when Zanuck announced his plans to put Grable in a nonmusical, but he was determined to pair her with his favorite leading man of the forties, the dashing Tyrone Power. Billie Grable strongly disapproved of the movie, considering *R.A.F.* a career mistake. She put aside all of her objections, however, after she met Ty Power and fell under the spell of his remarkable charm.

"I don't know why Betty doesn't fall in love with him," she murmured to her older daughter, Marjorie. "How do you know she hasn't already," Marjorie cracked, only too well aware her sister and Power were already sleeping together. The romance ended as soon as the production was completed, and Marjorie, by way of explanation, piped, "I guess Betty just wore him out."

Betty would relate the real reason years later to her closest friends. With time, the feminine odors had only worsened, which could not have pleased her young lover. After more frustrating visits to her physician, he one day—upon painstaking examination—discovered the cause of Betty's problem. He slowly removed a condom that had been lodged inside her—unnoticed by Power.

Alice Faye, too, had once been in love with Power. When once asked why she didn't marry him, she replied: "There were two reasons. First, he never asked me, and second, he liked boys too much."

*A Yank in the R.A.F.* went on to become one of the most popular films of 1941. Betty's excellent handling of the script bore out Zanuck's prediction that she would one day be recognized for her dramatic talents. Though her career as a dramatic actress was to be short-lived, critics unanimously hailed her performance as well focused and sharply drawn.

The 1940s marked the heyday of the Hollywood studios. Their powerful publicity departments had the clout to create legendary sex-symbols—Lana Turner was The Sweater Girl, Greta Garbo The Face, Ann Sheridan The Oomph Girl, Dorothy Lamour The Sarong Girl, and Marie McDonald The Body.

Someone in the publicity department at Fox hit upon an idea to promote a phony beauty contest and proclaim Betty Grable a winner in the "best legs" competition. From then on, her legs were known as "one of the most treasured assets of America," insured by Lloyd's of London for $1 million. In time all of her publicity focused on the legs: they measured 7½ inches at the ankles, 12 inches at the calf, with 18½-inch thighs, and a size 5 shoe. Her figure measured 34-23-35. The Fox publicity department busied itself with the fabrication of yet another love goddess: The Pin-Up Girl.

Taking a break from college, Marjorie came to Hollywood for a visit with her sister and mother. One night, while Betty prepared for a date, the toilet backed up. A short while later Marjorie let in a tall, timid, thin man who could not have been less prepossessing. Assuming he was the plumber, she offered: "If you'll follow me I'll show you where the bathroom is." The shy man stammered: "I'm here to pick up Miss Grable—I'm Howard Hughes."

"Betty didn't click with the elusive Hughes," Marjorie explained, "because she always refused the casting couch." It was true. She was never drawn to men who were merely wealthy. Nor was she ever deeply enthralled with the "Hollywood Handsomes"—Ty Power, Robert Stack, Desi Arnaz, Sr., Victor Mature, or Don Ameche—though they were all at some point physically drawn to *her*.

Robert Stack admits: "Betty was my first bout with unrequited love; it was a doozie. I fell, or thought I fell, for Betty Grable. She had already been married to Jackie Coogan . . . so I must have been as exciting to her as a bowl of Jell-O. I was so awed by having a date with my first real movie star. I took her out and treated her like the girl next door—a way in which even the girl next door doesn't want to be treated. I also gave her a love bauble, a gold heart with the notes and lyrics of 'I've Got a Crush on You' engraved all over it."

Betty preferred domineering, well-endowed macho men who were strong, independent, and good lovers—and who were generally not very handsome by Hollywood standards. All of them demonstrated a peculiar indifference to her beauty. She in turn tried to emasculate them; a compulsion learned firsthand from her mother. When they fled her tyranny, she turned to gay fans and chorus boys for solace, companionship, and sometimes, sex.

Betty wanted her father to be strong, to stand up to her mother and fight back during Billie's harangues. The complexities of her parents' relationship left her with a distorted perception of adult love and femininity. She could not have been more ill equipped to survive as a star in the male-chauvinist film industry. On every issue from contracts to costumes she eschewed her alluring femininity and chose her mother's weapon, abrasive confrontation.

From their first date in 1931—when she was fifteen and he thirty-six—George Raft had kept a close eye on Betty as she matured into a great beauty and a major star. In 1940, Raft approached Jack Benny's wife Mary Livingstone, a close friend of Betty's, and asked her to arrange a meeting with Betty at Ciro's. A highly publicized courtship ensued, tough-guy Raft showering Betty with lavish jewels, furs, and—in belated fulfillment of a childhood dream—a racehorse. For three years Betty was his obsession. As he began to take over her life, he fell into the complicated role of being a father to her. Unfortunately Raft misconstrued Billie's oppressive management of Betty as a demonstration of motherly devotion rather than what it actually was, the manipulation of a woman consumed by stardom.

"There was a time," Betty said, "when I told him I'd take my mother to dinner on the maid's night out. Once told was enough for George. From then on he never forgot that, and every Thursday night he asked my mother to be with us. George left nothing to be desired in the way of old-fashioned gallantry and chivalry."

Betty faced one serious problem as she struggled to get Raft to marry her—his wife, the former Grayce Mulrooney, from whom he'd been separated for twenty years. The oldest of ten children, Raft was born in 1895 to Italian-German parents in New York's Hell's Kitchen, a few blocks from Broadway. Because his father was a cold and distant man, Raft's mother, Eva, turned to her favorite son and showered him with affection. In reciprocating her devotion, Raft incurred his father's contempt.

Raft always referred to his self-sacrificing "Mom" in a hushed and reverent tone, noting how chaste, religious, and devoted she was as mother and wife. "Mom and I would dance together for hours," he said. "In fact, later on, when I became a dancer and entered a lot of dance contests, my mother would sometimes be my partner. We were a great team. I could've been the first X-rated dancer. I was very erotic. I used to caress myself as I danced. I never felt I was a great dancer. I was more of a stylist—unique. I was never Fred Astaire or Gene Kelly, but I was sensuous."

During his rise as a nightclub dancer, his mother encouraged him to marry. George believed "there were two kinds of girls in those days. Those who did, and those who didn't." He agreed to marry the girl of his mother's dreams—the seemingly virtuous Grayce Mulrooney. On their wedding night Grayce tearfully admitted she was not a virgin. George was shattered. "I thought Grayce was completely different," he said. "My wife was like any other broad I had been with. I felt tricked. I felt rejected and depressed."

The cuckolded bridegroom, still smarting from the unconsummated wedding night, awoke the next morning and sat down to write Mom. As he enclosed his usual $100 bill, Grayce protested. "My mother comes first!" he screamed. A separation followed but Mom eventually persuaded him to return to his wife.

"Grayce put on this negligee," he remembered. "I couldn't see it but I could feel it. One thing led to another and we began to make—let's call it love. It was ridiculous. The first and last time I made love to my so-called wife, I was blind drunk." Again they separated. But never divorced.

During the period of Raft's courting Betty, he would routinely escort her home from a night on the town, plant a kiss on her cheek, and then dash off to join his buddies for a round of all-night poker.

After two frustrating years of chaste love with Raft, Betty began flirting openly with other men to arouse his jealousy and stir him to action. Instead Raft beat her up. Betty had been warned by her studio bosses that Raft's links with the underworld were bad for her reputation; he was often seen at the races with mobster Bugsy Siegel. The aura of glamour, sex, and crime surrounding the Grable–Raft romance enraptured the American press and public, who made Betty and George the most celebrated couple of the early 1940s. Not until Elizabeth Taylor and Richard Burton in the sixties would there be anything like it.

Betty's box-office power soared. As such she became a household name and she was crowned by *The Harvard Lampoon* as "the worst actress to give the most consistently bad performances." Proclamations like that devastated her. She announced to the world that what she wanted most was not a career but marriage with the "right guy." For that, she stated—and often—she would abandon all her successes in a moment.

By 1943 she had zoomed to the number-one box-office position, edging out veteran superstar Bob Hope and the ever-popular comedy duo, Bud Abbott and Lou Costello. Betty Grable became the first female star to take the coveted top spot. How, reporters asked, could Grable be the major U.S. movie star when she was not a top singer or actress?

"Maybe it's a wholesome quality or an American-girl quality," Betty speculated. "People write to me as if I were their sister or a friend." Though her modesty was becoming, the star hardly needed to apologize for her preeminence in the American film musical of the 1940s. Her brand of luscious vulnerability, later aped by Marilyn Monroe, gave songs like "I Can't Begin to Tell You," "The More I See You," and "I Had the Craziest Dream" a soft, beguiling charm both original and tenderly moving. As a hoofer she moved with a pert sexiness, delightful and sassily provocative. But Betty continued to present herself as an ordinary person with little talent who just happened to have exceptional legs and good luck. Publicists would learn how to exploit her inferiority complex, transforming it into an unassuming persona that made Grable's approach to stardom seem uniquely refreshing. Her insecurity, though a useful gimmick that would endear her to millions of fans, was unfortunately held in deadly earnest by Betty.

Long since weary of the Hollywood scene, Grable was fed up with conditions at home. As the sole support of her mother, father, and two aunts, she now had the added burden of supporting her sister, Marjorie, her new husband, David, and their son, Peter, who had all come to California during the difficult wartime years. When President Roosevelt proposed that persons earning more than $25,000 a year be temporarily subjected to a salary freeze, Betty, upon being asked by a reporter what she thought of the proposed plan, said, "Well, you'd better ask all my relatives what they think of it first."

With Los Angeles full of servicemen, the Hollywood Canteen became the most glittering spot in town. Betty volunteered her services and soon became a regular. One night she met bandleader Harry James at the Canteen and began dating him—secretly, because she was still involved with George Raft. Betty was delighted to learn at Fox that she and Harry James would be working together in *Springtime in the Rockies*.

Though Betty had top billing, Carmen Miranda, with her wacky Brazilian version of "Chattanooga Choo Choo," stole the show. And Harry James also made a strong impression, reintroducing his hit "I Had the Craziest Dream," now featuring the voice of Helen Forrest. The song would later become Harry and Betty's theme song whenever they appeared together onstage or in night clubs.

Frank Powolny, Fox's still photographer, snapped a legendary photo of Carmen Miranda. It was never released publicly, but it enjoyed great notoriety in Hollywood and remains sought after even today by film collectors. Powolny was photographing Miranda with dance partner Cesar Romero for *Springtime in the Rockies* stills. Though Miranda was always cooperative, she had failed to appear for her photo sessions. Under pressure from his immediate supervisors, and with only one day left before his vacation, Powolny asked Romero to please see to it that Miss Miranda appeared for the next day's session.

It was a hot, windless July day—before the advent of air-conditioning—when Powolny, under the sweltering heat of glaring studio lights, began to set up his cameras. Romero was dressed in a tuxedo and Miranda wore a skirt with a long slit from the floor to just below her navel and a mile-high turban of plastic cherries, apricots, and bananas on her head. Romero swooped Miranda up and twirled her about as Powolny snapped a roll of film. On his return from vacation, Powolny discovered himself in the midst of a studio uproar over the photographs. In one of the shots, Miranda, caught in all her "*Cuanto le gusta*" abandonment, was suspended in midair—with no panties on.

When Powolny later photographed Betty Grable in her Hawaiian grass skirt costume for *Song of the Islands,* she looked him straight in the eye and deadpanned, "Well, Frankie—at least I've got my panties on!"

# CHAPTER 7

Though falling in love with Harry was easy to do, Betty discovered breaking up with Raft was fraught with danger. She feared Raft's close underworld connections and convinced Harry they should continue to conceal their liaison from him.

Raft spied on Grable. He solicited the services of two cronies, Ben Platt and former boxer Mac Gray, telling them to follow her and report back to him on a daily basis. Raft was able to keep abreast of all her activities, including her affair with Harry. One night, after Betty and Harry retired to the upstairs back bedroom of her home, the couple was startled by a loud crash followed by a series of shouts and groans. Looking out the window they saw Platt and Gray scamper off, having toppled from their perch in a tree.

Betty and Harry decided to go public with their romance. While she was sitting with Harry in a Hollywood nightclub where his band was performing, Raft walked up to Betty shouting obscenities and accusing her of cheating. Alarmed by the prospect of scandal, Betty firmly asked him to leave her alone. Raft completely lost control and smacked Harry James in the mouth. A full-scale fistfight broke out. Though Raft was an amateur boxer, he was no match for the younger, stronger, and taller James. The brawl made the headlines in the next morning's papers, which were filled with pictures and lengthy eyewitness accounts. Fought over by a dashing matinee idol and the leader of the nation's hottest band, Betty Grable instantly turned into the reigning sex symbol of her time.

She loved being the focus of attention and was flattered by Harry's chivalry. Harry seemed the man she had been waiting for. "He's easy to be with," she told Billie. "It's relaxing to be with him." She set her goal: marriage. Harry, however, was still married, and former band singer Louise Tobin, the mother of his two sons, had no intention of divorcing him.

Betty decided to announce to the world that her "love affair" with Raft was over. She chose as her forum the column of powerful Hearst columnist Louella Parsons, who was naturally ecstatic over the exclusive. "I would have married George a week after I met him," Betty said. "But when you wait two and a half years, there doesn't seem to be any future in romance with a married man." Parsons noted tears in Betty's eyes. "I don't expect to get over George today, tomorrow, or next week. But I do know there's no turning back. I never exercise a woman's privilege of changing her mind."

Betty admitted to a friend her relationship with Raft—the press still called it "The Love Affair of the Forties"—was in fact platonic. She suspected "George was probably a latent homosexual." After his separation from Grayce Mulrooney, he never married again. In later years Betty characterized him as "one of the kindest and most generous men I have ever met."

Chance played the crucial role in Betty Grable's career. After her impressive dramatic debut in *A Yank in the R.A.F.*, released in 1941, Darryl Zanuck was determined to develop her as Fox's leading dramatic actress. But as unprecedented box-office receipts started pouring in from the musical comedy *Down Argentine Way*, released only a year earlier, in 1940, the studio recognized a new South American market for U.S. films. World War II had destroyed the European market, which at one time had accounted for half of the industry's grosses. Zanuck shrewdly decided to reach out to the neighboring Latin American countries. In the process he created a new musical comedy genre.

*Down Argentine Way*, the picture that brought Grable back to Hollywood, ended her dramatic career before it got started. But the movie made Betty Grable and Carmen Miranda leading stars of the wartime years. Audiences and critics loved the film's outrageous sense of camp. Bosley Crowther of *The New York Times* wrote, "Offhand, we can't think of anyone more abundantly qualified to serve as a mini-actress plenipotentiary to the Latin American lands than Betty Grable."

Betty's costar in *Down Argentine Way* was supposed to be Desi Arnaz, Sr. Desi was involved with Lucille Ball, an old friend of Betty's. "She was gorgeous," Arnaz recalls about Betty. "What a figure, and what legs! Her skin was magnificent and so smooth—she looked like a peach all over. It was impossible to sit next to her and not want to know her a little better." For personal reasons, Arnaz was forced to turn down the picture. The part went to Don Ameche, a very popular leading man at Fox, though not a Latin type.

Zanuck spotted Carmen Miranda, the "Brazilian Bombshell," already a major recording star in her adopted Rio de Janeiro, in the Broadway musical *Streets of Paris*. He immediately signed her for a featured role in *Down Argentine Way*. Miranda's producer refused to release her from her stage contract. Undeterred, Zanuck sent a crew to New York to film all of Miranda's musical sequences. Despite her featured billing, Carmen Miranda did not deliver a single spoken word of dialogue. Miranda and Grable were to appear together again in *Springtime in the Rockies*, released the year after Betty's dramatic triumph in *A Yank in the R.A.F.*

Enormously pleased with Betty's popularity after *Down Argentine Way*, Zanuck decided to take personal command of her career. He quickly cast her in the role of Alice Faye's sister in *Tin Pan Alley*, a non-Technicolor musical about struggling songwriters in New York City during World War I. Grable's big song was "When You Wore a Tulip and I Wore a Big Red Rose." But it was her elaborately mounted, risqué "Sheik of Araby" production number with Alice Faye that turned *Tin Pan Alley* into the box-office hit of the year. Dressed in see-through harem pants, Grable and Faye shimmied and shook for the sheik, played by comedian Billy Gilbert. Betty's spectacular photogenic appeal easily stole the spotlight from the two veteran players. Audiences cheered the sexually explicit scene that somehow managed to slip through the censor's office, probably because Gilbert's slapstick mugging served as comic relief for the steamier stuff.

By the end of 1940, Faye, a personal favorite of Zanuck's, and his original choice for the lead in *Down Argentine Way*, had reportedly grown tired of her career, opting instead to retire and settle down with musician husband Phil Harris and their two daughters. The real reason for her sudden departure from Fox: she was fed up with Zanuck's tyrannical demands and his constant manipulations and interference with her personal life. The Fox musical crown passed from Alice Faye to Betty Grable for keeps, even as *A Yank in the R.A.F.* hit the theaters, followed shortly by Betty's very good dramatic performance in the minor film classic *I Wake Up Screaming*. Betty was never to play another straight dramatic lead on film.

At the age of fifteen, Zanuck, an eighth-grade dropout, joined the U.S. Army; he was posted in Deming, New Mexico. Under General "Black Jack" Pershing, who had already been in and out of Mexico in pursuit of Pancho Villa, Zanuck reportedly fought in one or two of the skirmishes with the Mexican rebel leader.

Zanuck went to work for Warner Bros., moving his way up to story editor and finally production chief. Recognizing the potential of the musical as a film genre, he put his future on the line with *42nd Street*, a major success that solidified his reputation as a boy genius.

20th Century Films was formed in 1933 by Zanuck and Joseph Schenck. Their films were released by United Artists, whose people were viewed by both Zanuck and Schenck as money grabbers. At the same time, William Fox of Fox Film Corporation needed financial assistance; because Fox had the best distribution system in the movie business, Schenck offered a merger package deal to Fox, which was actually headed by Sidney Kent.

Zanuck was thirty-three when he was named head of 20th Century–Fox. He inherited a roster of stars, many of whom he didn't like and others who he felt would not fit into his plans at Fox. He harbored a strong dislike for the "ladylike" stars, Janet Gaynor and Loretta Young, both of whom he thought demanding and aggressive. They soon left Fox.

The well-built five-foot five-inch tycoon often appeared on the lot dressed in riding jodhpurs and knee-high boots. He carried a riding crop that he beat on his desk or against his boot to emphasize a point. He constantly chewed on a long cigar. Zanuck had a rule: all his female stars were to warm his bed. "Every afternoon," a former employee remembered, "Zanuck had to have his virility assured. But neither Betty Grable nor Alice Faye ever slept with Darryl Zanuck."

One of Zanuck's most eccentric edicts was that his male stars should never have hair on their chests. Zanuck told Gilbert Roland he would have to shave his chest before signing a contract with Fox. "I don't shave my chest for anybody," Roland said. "Do you know what that feels like when it begins to grow out?"

"You don't show any hair on your chest in my films," Zanuck barked.

"You take your film and shove it, because I'm not going to shave my chest!"

"That's the door," Zanuck thundered. "You're not going to do the film." Roland stormed out.

Ty Power, a Zanuck favorite, was blessed with a hairless chest. The hirsute John Payne, another Zanuck protegé, never objected to the discomforting ordeal of shaving his chest for the boss. Nor would William Holden, years later, in *Love Is a Many-Splendored Thing*.

Zanuck, behind the locked door of his studio office, would flash for his starlets and speak of his manhood as if it were a work of art. "Isn't it beautiful?" he asked Grable during her first months at Fox. "Yes," she said, "and you can put it away now."

In 1942, after the release of *Song of the Islands,* Betty's fan mail zoomed to 1,000 letters a week. Theater owners across the country placed her among the top ten box-office draws. By the next year, she would be No. 1. Zanuck guaranteed that all her future projects would be big-budget Technicolor movies. One important bet Zanuck missed with Grable: he refused to let her record any of the songs she made famous, mistakenly thinking the public, hearing Grable on the radio, would not bother to see her films. Zanuck was wrong. In the late forties, under the assumed name of Ruth Haag, Grable had a great hit with Harry James in "I Can't Begin to Tell You." She could have been a major recording star all along.

In the pin-up photo that made her the most famous—and the highest paid—woman in the world, Betty Grable stands in all her peaches-and-cream glory, dressed simply in a one-piece backless white bathing suit, high-heeled white satin baby-dolls, and a thin gold ankle chain that was a gift from George Raft. With her hair in the upswept style she popularized in the forties and her back to the camera, her hands rest loosely on slim hips. Chin pressing coyly against a raised right shoulder, Betty Grable stares teasingly into the camera lens. With her slightly curved, boyish slim body, Grable redefined femininity and helped usher in the first wave of the sexual revolution of the century.

The unorthodox derriere pose dealt a fatal blow to the smoldering, arched sexuality of the 1930s. Then, the feminine ideal was personified by hippy, voluptuous, large-breasted women like Jean Harlow. Betty's no-nonsense, what-you-see-is-what-you-get brand of sexuality epitomized the new American female—not only for men but for the newly emancipated wartime working woman who had only recently joined a male-dominated workforce. Betty's fresh-flesh, flirty-fun sex appeal released a flood of new social habits, but none more widespread than the teenage craze for dating and jitterbug dancing to big-band swing.

The public embraced Grable's image as a welcome relief from the "heavy" female stars of the era—neurotic Bette Davis, sincere Greer Garson, dangerous Lana Turner, sacred Ingrid Bergman, tragic Greta Garbo, severe Joan Crawford, and exotic Hedy Lamarr—all of whom struggled and wept through a maze of wartime films. Betty's alternately brash and breathy sensuality enraptured a wide and divergent range of fans: including a million servicemen, their wives, children, sisters, mothers, and even their grandmothers.

Hundreds of millions of copies of the pin-up circulated throughout the world; many were found even in the packs of captured Japanese and German soldiers also addicted to the American pin-up queen. Sentimental World War II veterans and their families approached Betty throughout the rest of her life to pay their respects to her for helping them make it through the duration. "There we were," a veteran once said to Betty, "out in those damn dirty trenches. Machine guns firing. Bombs dropping all around us. We would be exhausted, frightened, confused and sometimes hopeless about our situation, when suddenly someone would pull your picture out of his wallet. Or we'd see a decal of you on a plane and then we'd *know* what we were fighting for."

Rita Hayworth's sweetly seductive *Life* spread ran a poor second to the Grable pin-up during World War II. Rita crouched on her knees, in bed, dressed in a lacy black negligee. Not until Marilyn Monroe's scandalous nude calendar photo in the fifties would anything equal the impact of Betty's pin-up. And nothing since, except, perhaps, Sophia Loren's *Boy on a Dolphin* photo displaying her breasts in a wet dress.

Frank Powolny, who took the salacious Carmen Miranda photo, snapped the immortal Grable pin-up. "It was 1941," he related, "during the summertime, before Pearl Harbor. That's when we shot the picture. I only made two. I didn't shoot it in color. It was the early days before color. As we finished the poses I asked Betty, 'How about some back shots?'

"'Like this?' Betty asked.

"'That's what I want—it's exactly what I want.'"

The first shot didn't have the hard swing of the body toward the camera that Powolny knew he wanted. He requested a second shot, and that's the one that made history. "That's all it was—just a posed shot. We didn't know it was to be used for such enormous publicity." Fox publicists told the press Betty had said, "Okay, Frank, you've got the camera and I've got the figure." Dancer Jeff Parker, who would later become intimate with Grable, remembered yet another version of the fateful photo session. "The only reason she looked over her shoulder," he said, "was because she was pregnant. She *couldn't* turn around. Her stomach was sticking out. Powolny said, 'Just turn around and look over your shoulder.' Betty said, 'I kept talking about my stomach during the photo session. I was worried about my stomach.'"

After the pin-up became a World War II classic, Powolny photographed Betty many more times, but she never referred to the famous still. Grable held to a strict rule: never more than one shot of any one pose. She personally counted each shot Powolny snapped. Shortly after the photo session Grable underwent her second abortion. When asked to comment on her apparent pregnancy the dignified Powolny replied: "It wasn't that far away . . . It wasn't that far . . ."

# CHAPTER 8

Betty Grable was five weeks pregnant when Harry James's wife agreed to a quickie Mexican divorce. Betty and Harry arranged to meet in Las Vegas for their wedding, a halfway point between New York, where James was playing, and Los Angeles, where Grable's absence would hold up the start of her next film, *Pin-Up Girl*. Critic James Agee wrote: "During the making of *Pin-Up Girl*, Betty Grable was in the early stages of pregnancy; everyone else was evidently in a late stage of paresis."

The couple arranged to be married in a little church on the grounds of the Frontier Hotel on July 5, 1943. The ceremony would be followed by a private and dignified reception. Despite the secrecy surrounding the event, word soon leaked to Fox publicity. The studio dispatched Frank Powolny to cover the ceremony. Although Frank and Betty were friends, Fox told him not to disclose his business to Betty. But Betty spotted him on the rickety wartime train to Vegas.

"Frank, what are you doing here?"

"I'm going on a trip."

"Frank, what the *hell* are you up to?"

"I have to tell you—I'm photographing your wedding."

"What wedding?" she said, winking at him. Betty allowed Powolny to trail her and even offered him, later, exclusive photos of herself with James following the wedding.

Harry's train arrived several hours late. Tired, tense, and chain-smoking, Betty waited in a limousine, surrounded by fans and photographers in a carnival mood. Harry alighted from the train and made a dash for the limo, tripping and falling as photographers snapped away.

The couple drove to the Baptist Little Church of the West. It was 4:00 A.M. Awaiting them as they arrived was their witness, Betty Furness, as well as hundreds of shrieking fans and blazing floodlights reminiscent of a Hollywood premiere. Outraged, Betty and Harry pushed through the crowds, ignoring mikes hooked up to loudspeakers. Vegas newspapers attacked the "Hollywood aliens" for their "tasteless lack of proper behavior. Go back to Tinseltown." Though still smarting from the press fiasco around the Coogan scandals, Grable decided to temper her public response. In her best unblinking and wide-eyed manner, she told the press, "I'm really grateful for the many thoughtful comments by the Las Vegas press," and went on to assure that she would always view the citizens of Las Vegas as her "friends."

There was no honeymoon, but Betty didn't care. She had found her perfect man, a virile trumpet player. From now on, she preferred the company of other musicians to Hollywood "phonies." She said, "It would be very romantic if I could say that love came like a trumpet blast to Harry and me—except that it didn't. I first heard him play at the College Inn in Chicago, when I was working a personal appearance at the Chicago Theatre. Actually I'd gone to the Inn to hear Dick Haymes who was singing with him then and whom I knew. I was going with someone else at the time, and to me Harry was just the man on the end of the horn—and a *married man* at that. It happened to be the sweetest horn I'd ever heard, however, and after that I'd rush over to the Inn every night after my last show, with my mother."

Harry James was in his prime—universally regarded as the greatest trumpet player in the world. Handsome, tall, and sleek, the mustachioed "stud," as Grable referred to him, was considered very sexy by the public. His music, which drew millions of young Americans to the dance halls, made him a popular choice as the consort for America's No. 1 glamour girl. During World War II the handsome pair ruled the worlds of pop music and movies—they were the focus of fan magazines, weekly periodicals, daily newspapers, and radio broadcasts across the country. Superficially Betty and Harry had much in common. Both grew up in show business and both shared a variety of sports interests—baseball, bowling, horses, horse racing, gambling. Most important, they shared a deep loathing for Hollywood.

Harry Haag James was born in Albany, Georgia, on March 15, 1916, the same year as Grable. The only child of circus performers, Everette and Maybelle James, Harry grew up under the Big Top. Everette was band director for the Mighty Haag Circus, and Maybelle, an aerial artist, the foremost circus prima donna. She stunned audiences with her death-defying act, "The Iron Jaw." She continued to work the high wires through eight months of pregnancy, stopping just long enough to give birth to Harry. Maybelle went back on the job when Harry was just twelve days old. His childhood bore some uncanny similarities to Betty's. Everette wanted a show-business career for his son. For the first fifteen years of his life Harry performed in the circus, starting at age four as a contortionist. He did everything from dressing up as Cinderella to playing the drums in the circus band before he took up the trumpet by age eight.

By 1931, the James family had retired from the circus and settled in Beaumont, Texas, where Everette became a public school music supervisor. After graduating from high school, Harry started playing gigs with local bands in nearby Galveston and in Dallas. It was in Dallas that jazz great Ben Pollack first heard Harry James and hired him for his band. In the 1935 Pollack recording of "Deep Elm," James's trumpet work attracted the attention of Benny Goodman, who brought him to New York. Harry was nineteen when he met singer Louise Tobin and got married. In 1939, with Goodman's blessing and a $5,000 advance, Harry left the band to form his own.

On New Year's Day 1942, after appearing at the Stanley Theatre in Pittsburgh, twenty-five-year-old Harry received his first critical acclaim and began to amass a huge following among teenagers. His success brought Harry a Hollywood contract, and though his first film flopped, his recording of "You Made Me Love You" made him a major recording star. The song, closely associated with Al Jolson and later Judy Garland, was by far the most commercially successful when rendered by Harry James. "I always liked to listen to Judy sing it," he said. "And none of us figured the record would be big."

Though his film career fizzled, James went on to great successes with many recordings and nightclub appearances. He is credited with launching the careers of Frank Sinatra, Dick Haymes, and Helen Forrest.

Harry James had fathered two sons by the time he met and married Betty Grable.

Victoria Elizabeth James, called Vicki, came into the world on March 3, 1944, at 4:45 A.M. in Cedars of Lebanon Hospital. Named after the character Betty played in *Springtime in the Rockies*, "The Little Pin-Up," as the press tagged her, was born eight months after the wedding. The birth was an extremely difficult one: Betty labored seventeen hours before submitting to a cesarean section.

Requests for the first baby pictures inundated the Fox publicity department. In September 1944 *Life* magazine, the most widely read periodical in the world, published a full-color pin-up photograph of Betty's baby lying on her stomach, nude, legs kicking behind her as she flashed a million-dollar smile.

Three years later, Betty announced she was pregnant again. "If it's a girl," she bubbled, "her name will be Jessica. And if it's a boy, he will be named Harry Haag James for his father.

Baby Betty, seven months old in 1917, plays in the garden at her parents' home in St. Louis.
*Courtesy The Bettmann Archive.*

• • •

Betty's certificate of baptism into the Episcopal Church.
*Photo The Museum of Modern Art Film Stills Archives.*

**In the Name of The Father,**
**And of The Son, and of The Holy Ghost. Amen.**

**We do Certify:**

That, according to the ordinance of Christ Himself, we did administer to

Elizabeth Ruth [Grable]

THE SACRAMENT OF

**Holy Baptism**

thereby making Her a Member of Christ, the Child of God, and an Inheritor of the Kingdom of Heaven; on the twenty sixth day of March, in the Year of our Lord, One Thousand Nine Hundred and twenty-one; the said administration being in St. John's Church, St. Louis, in the Diocese of Missouri

(Signed) William A. Stimpson

Parents: John C. Grable; Lillian H. Grable

Sponsors or Witnesses: Estelle Grable; Rebecca Grable; Houston Hill

Date of Birth Dec. 18, 1916

As early as age three and a half, Betty was poised and ready for the camera.
*Courtesy The Bettmann Archive.*

Eleven-year-old Betty about to ham it up in blackface.
*Courtesy The Bettmann Archive.*

• • •

Betty (*center*), at twelve, poses with two models. Already in a bathing suit.
*Courtesy The Bettmann Archive.*

Betty (*left*) and the Rocky Twins.
*Photo The Museum of Modern Art Film Stills Archives/20th Century–Fox.*

• • • • • •

Betty (*left*) and her sister, Marjorie (Mrs. David Arnold), eight years her senior, take a break from riding in this 1930 photo. As a child, Betty begged her mother, Billie, for a horse of her own.
*Photo The Museum of Modern Art Film Stills Archives.*

• • • • •

A musical Betty, with Jimmy Durante and Maxine Doyle at the Douville Beach Club in 1934.
*Photo The Museum of Modern Art Film Stills Archives.*

• • • • •

(*Left to right*) Coy Poe, Dixie Dunbar, Jackie Coogan, Betty Grable, Toni Brown, and Phyllis Frazer take a bow in 1936.
*Photo The Museum of Modern Art Film Stills Archives.*

Lana Turner (*left*) and Anne Shirley (*center*) celebrate with Betty at a bridal shower in 1937 for her impending marriage to former child star Jackie Coogan. *Photo The Museum of Modern Art Film Stills Archives.*

• • •

Betty and Jackie cut the cake at the wedding reception held in their honor at Betty's home. *Photo The Museum of Modern Art Film Stills Archives.*

COLLEGE SWING

Words by FRANK LOESSER Music by HOAGY CARMICHAEL

Adolph Zukor presents

COLLEGE SWING

GEORGE BURNS and GRACIE ALLEN
MARTHA RAYE
BOB HOPE
EDWARD E. HORTON
BEN BLUE
BETTY GRABLE
JACKIE COOGAN
FLORENCE GEORGE
JOHN PAYNE
SKINNAY ENNIS
Directed by RAOUL WALSH
A PARAMOUNT PICTURE

FAMOUS MUSIC CORPORATION · 1619 B'WAY · NEW YORK CITY

• • •

Betty paid her dues making a series of B-grade college-swing pictures before hitting it big. *Courtesy Famous Music Corporation Paramount Pictures.*

The pin-up girl with the million-dollar legs turned heads long before the legendary 1941 pose.
*Photo The Museum of Modern Art Film Stills Archives/20th Century–Fox.*

• • • • •

*The Day the Bookies Wept* (1939) would be a prophetic film for Betty, considering the hard luck she would have later in life with her own gambling....
*Photo The Museum of Modern Art Film Stills Archives-RKO Radio Pictures, Inc.*

• • •

Betty with her new boyfriend, Artie Shaw, shortly after her divorce from Jackie Coogan in October 1939. To reports that she might marry Artie, Betty answered, "That's a lot of bunk." But she was angry when he rejected her proposal in favor of Lana Turner!
*Courtesy Wide World Photos, Inc.*

• • •

• • •

Alice Faye, acknowledged "Queen of the 20th Century–Fox Musicals," and a young Betty strumming ukuleles in *Tin Pan Alley* (1940).
*Courtesy The Bettmann Archive 20th Century–Fox.*

Jessie James wouldn't be so cute for a boy. It could be taken seriously."

Jessie James, a girl, was born five weeks premature at Cedars of Lebanon. Her birth—even more difficult than Victoria's—seemed a bad omen to the superstitious Betty. She was disappointed Jessie was not a boy and said angrily that she'd never get pregnant again.

Working in Atlantic City, Harry James could not be reached by telephone. Betty, enraged by Harry's seeming indifference, vented her anger on the doctors, nurses, and even her mother. Billie scolded and nagged Betty for having allowed herself to become pregnant, thereby interrupting her career. "Don't ever," Billie warned, "*ever* do this to *me* again."

"And she never did," Jessica would say years later, remembering that her mother often complained about the terrible and lonely night she was born. Jessica's difficult delivery was termed placenta praevia, an uncommon delivery in which the afterbirth blocks the exit from the uterus and causes severe hemorrhaging, often necessitating removal of the fetus by cesarean section. Ironically, Jessica herself, many years later, experienced the same complications when she gave birth. Because placenta praevia is not a congenital condition, the anomaly was considered so rare it was documented and later recorded in the *Medical Books of Records*.

A musician friend of Harry's recalled that James also expressed disappointment the child was not a boy; the son he hoped for.

"What's really important in a marriage," Betty told reporters, "is the way you feel about each other and the way you get along. We're deeply in love, Harry and I. It's a funny thing with us that just grows and grows."

To Hedda Hopper she confided: "Luckily both Harry and I measure up to about the same place in different fields. That's wonderful because he's so sensitive that way. I can be Mrs. James, all right—but he could never, never be Mr. Grable." But in fact, Betty Grable, the highest-paid actress in the world, set an impossible standard for Harry, whose salary, even during his peak years, never exceeded $50,000—hardly enough to cover his drinking and gambling. When marital difficulties surfaced, Betty steadfastly blamed Harry's work on the road because it kept him away from home ninety percent of the time. In desperation, Betty joined him on tour. But it didn't work. The audience was distracted by her presence. The musicians in the band, unimpressed with her celebrity, froze her out of their family-like camaraderie. To avoid upstaging her proud and sensitive husband, Betty tried sneaking into the dance halls alone, where she would sit at a remote table and watch her man, unobserved. During these lonely nights, isolated among thousands of jubilant revelers, Betty acquired two lethal habits, cigarette smoking and drinking. On the surface, at least, it appeared stars Harry and Betty had much in common, with their shared enthusiasm for sports, horse racing, and gambling, and even their contempt for the Hollywood social scene. But Betty failed to admit, even to herself, one very important fact—Harry, addicted gambler that he was, was simply incapable of loving anyone. Despite her own dismal history of failed loves and romances, Betty chose to ignore all the warning signals of an unworkable marriage. Throughout her life, she deluded herself that Harry was the only man for her.

She eventually conceded that her place was at home and settled for Harry's nightly long-distance phone calls. Grable used her power at Fox to persuade Zanuck to cast Harry in *Kitten on the Keys,* a movie so terrible it had to be scrapped and filmed again. This time as *Do You Love Me?* it was still so bad Fox withdrew it from distribution. Harry played a trumpet player who fell in love with a female college dean, Maureen O'Hara, only to lose her in the end to Dick Haymes. Incensed over an ending that portrayed her husband as a loser, Grable demanded a gag finale. James, after leaving O'Hara, climbs into a car where he finds the real Betty Grable, arms outstretched.

Even these efforts failed to keep the marriage alive. Betty, in desperation, blamed Zanuck for her husband's acting failures as well as her problems at home. Zanuck attempted to mollify his top box-office draw by letting her approve her costars for *The Dolly Sisters.* Though she wanted Dick Haymes, Zanuck reportedly denied her request because he disapproved of their relationship. Instead, he submitted Perry Como for her final approval, but she felt that he was "too short" and finally agreed to casting John Payne. As for the other Dolly sister, the film's producer, George Jessel, said, "Alice Faye was never considered for the part though Zanuck [whom Jessel loathed] wanted her. Grable did not have final casting approval. I did." Of course, Faye had "retired" four years since after the filming of *Tin Pan Alley*. Jessel submitted June Haver for the role and Betty agreed, later regretting her acquiescence. June bore an uncanny resemblance to Betty as a peroxide blonde, though she was a bit shorter than Grable.

Charles LeMaire, Betty's costume designer, remembered that "Haver was definitely a different type of girl than *[sic]* Betty [alluding to her religious nature], and she didn't have the fight that Betty had." According to Betty's family and close friends, Betty knew better: she disliked June for two reasons—her ambitions and her insincere ladylike posture. "Betty could always spot a phony a mile away," Marjorie said.

Betty distrusted June, who often referred to the Bible as she expostulated on the sins of the flesh. Everyone on the set knew, as did Betty, that June was having an affair with George Jessel, who had a reputation for stalking blonde starlets. Betty also felt June was criticizing her around the studio. By now, 1945, Betty was undisputed queen of the Fox lot and well on her way to a reputation as a difficult and temperamental star.

One day June appeared at the set on time as usual. Betty was late. June, feigning innocence, pointedly asked for the time as a glaring reminder that the star was tardy. June was assured Betty would be along soon, prepared and ready to shoot. "Oh, that remains to be seen," she replied sweetly. That June and Betty avoided a major altercation was a tribute to Betty's professionalism. She said, "Nothing must interfere with the performance."

Noël Coward, struck by the physical similarity of the two blondes, quipped that Haver and Grable were actually the same person on a split screen and that *The Dolly Sisters* was Hollywood's way of solving the labor shortage.

At home, Betty was mired in problems created by a totally irresponsible husband. He assumed no role in raising or caring for his two daughters. He did not pay bills or manage the large household staff. He heaped gambling debts on Betty running into hundreds of thousands of dollars. He added insult to injury by flaunting his proclivity for showgirls. Harry publicly stated his priorities in the following order: "Music first, closely followed by baseball, horses, and then family life."

Betty's daily routine could scarcely have been grimmer. She awoke at 5:00 A.M. to leave for the studio before the girls got out of bed. Harry, meawhile, lay sleeping off a late-night dance gig followed by a poker game. When Grable returned at 10:00 P.M., the girls were already asleep and Harry was gone for the night. It was indeed ironic that the world's leading sex symbol spent all her nights alone. Shortly after the marriage, Betty and Harry began drifting apart as Harry's roadwork kept him away from home for longer and longer periods of time. Charles LeMaire found Betty understandably difficult on the set. He stated she lost interest in her career after Jessie's birth. LeMaire bore no great love for Betty, characterizing her as "extremely coarse." On the set of *Billy Rose's Diamond Horseshoe*, LeMaire called Betty back to the fitting room for final touches on a gown she particularly loved. When she tried it on, all hell broke loose. Grable stood cursing out the fitters when LeMaire walked in.

"What's the matter, dear?" he asked.

"The goddamn thing doesn't fit. What the hell happened? It couldn't have shrunk like that. What's the matter with you people in here? You took my best fitter away."

"Yes," confirmed the Academy Award–winning designer. "I made her head of Wardrobe and it was she who supervised your fitting."

"But she didn't *do* the fitting," Betty argued.

"I'll tell you the only thing wrong, Betty. And that's the bourbon with all the beer chasers you're drinking every night when Harry is gone. That's what's giving you those four-inch paunches around the waist."

"That has nothing to do with it. And besides, it's none of your business what I drink."

"It's my business to make a costume that fits your figure."

Travilla, another Oscar-winning designer, knew one of his fitters was mercilessly browbeaten by Grable. The fitter lived in a state of abject fear. Each time she delivered a costume to Betty she spit on the lower seam for good luck, hoping to avoid the star's rage.

Since her marriage to Harry James, Betty's weight had been fluctuating wildly. She'd always had a penchant for soft drinks and ice-cream sodas, but now, partying on occasion with musicians and gamblers who drank great quantities of booze, Betty was either hung over or grouchy from dieting. To shed enough pounds to fit into her tight and often scanty costumes, Grable often stopped drinking cold turkey and went on a strict high-protein diet of steak and eggs. In a few days she'd be her pin-up self again. Meanwhile, she was the scourge of Wardrobe as she taunted and intimidated the designers and fitters whom she considered weak. Betty was careful, however, not to treat her directors and cameramen the same way, as she knew too well that they could make or break a star. And her tantrums were not restricted to designers and fitters. Though she knew directors and cameramen can make or break a star, Betty Grable allowed herself to bully those she considered weak.

Just before filming *Diamond Horseshoe,* Zanuck announced a new director had been hired to replace the one originally set. The soft-spoken and gentle George Seaton would be making his directorial debut. Incensed, Betty stormed into Zanuck's office, demanding Seaton be fired. Zanuck overruled her. Betty started a relentless campaign to have Seaton removed, also attacked the producer, a publicity man, and LeMaire, claiming they were conspiring to sabotage her film. Zanuck called a meeting.

"Betty is not happy with the way the picture is going," he said. "She claims nobody pays any attention to her. No one is civil to her and she feels she's treated like a chorus girl." With some levity he added, "No one says good morning to her and no one says good night to her."

Seaton, LeMaire, and reportedly Harry Brand of the publicity department protested, claiming it was Betty who ignored *them,* refusing even to acknowledge their presence. Under the circumstances, how could they say, "Good morning, Miss Grable?"

"Just a minute," Zanuck cautioned. He summoned Betty from an adjoining room where she had been eavesdropping. "Betty, come in here."

*"Well,"* she pouted, seating herself next to the boss. "I just don't think I'm being treated like I should—I'm a star here and I want to be treated like one. Besides, the publicity is bad."

"What do you mean, it's bad?" demanded the publicist. "We can't get you when we want you. Anyway, we have a hard time keeping your name *out* of the paper, with you and your husband and those drunken brawls. You're fighting too much in public—"

Grable hastily changed the subject to the director. "Mr. Seaton doesn't understand me. He's never directed me before. Besides, they're making a director out of him on one of *my* pictures."

"Sorry I'm too young for you, Miss Grable," George Seaton said, "but I think the picture is coming along nicely. You look beautiful and you're acting very well."

"I'm not complaining about you," Grable backed off. Then she touched on the real issue. "I just wish *somebody* would pay a little more attention to me and say good morning to me and make me feel welcome."

The next morning, as Grable entered the soundstage, the entire cast and crew stopped in the middle of a scene and chorused in unison, *"Good morning, Miss Grable!"* She nodded her head in mock appreciation and proceeded to her dressing room.

Betty abandoned her manners whenever confronted with a strong person or authority figure. But if anyone could outshout her she immediately backed down. Few attempted confrontation, however, with the queen of Fox.

Motion picture academy president Howard W. Koch, who worked on *Diamond Horseshoe,* recounted that Betty once heard that a rumor was spreading among the film crew that she wore falsies. She rounded up the crew and confronted them on the set. "Okay," Grable deadpanned, hands on hips, "which one of you is spreading this lie about me wearing falsies?" When a gaffer stepped forward, Betty took his hand and placed it firmly on her breast. "Now," she laughed, "does that feel like a falsie?"

For once, the crew cheered Betty Grable.

*Billy Rose's Diamond Horseshoe* marks the apex of Betty's career; it was a dazzling vehicle tailored to display her showgirl glamour. "The More I See You" is perhaps the quintessential love song of a romantic, sentimental era, and her rendition of "In Acapulco" is Betty Grable at her good-natured, lovable best. It was 1945, the war was ending, and a jubilant nation had great fun watching its chosen screen sweetheart strut her gorgeous stuff.

# CHAPTER 9

By 1946, Betty was casting about for ways to sustain her popularity. With Billie's approval, she decided to soften her brassy showgirl persona. Henceforth, Grable announced, she would accept only those roles that presented her as "a mature woman." The result was *The Shocking Miss Pilgrim,* a flop.

The film was a forerunner of the women's liberation movement. Betty gave an intelligent performance as a late-nineteenth-century woman who makes it in the all-male legal secretary profession. But with the celebrated legs hidden under Victorian petticoats, fans rejected the new Grable, inundating Fox with 100,000 letters of protest.

At $150,000 per picture, Betty earned more than even Zanuck, her boss. Zanuck, convinced the time had come again for Betty to assume meatier, more dramatic roles, insisted she play a drunken kleptomaniac named Sophie in *The Razor's Edge.* Betty stubbornly refused. The lavishly produced Somerset Maugham classic went on to become one of the most popular and prestigious films of the year. The role Grable spurned went to Anne Baxter, who won the 1946 Academy Award as Best Supporting Actress.

Nunnally Johnson, screenwriter, producer, and director, quipped: "I don't know what Betty would want with an Oscar on her mantle when she has every Tom, Dick, and Harry at her feet." But her career, reeling from the *Miss Pilgrim* fiasco, could have used the challenge of the Sophie role—and the Oscar.

In private Grable anguished over the missed opportunity but braced herself and tried to mask her insecurities: "My movie lines up to now have consisted mostly of 'Hi, Joe' in musicals. Some of my parts required no acting ability. I didn't even study a script . . . I just worried about my hair and clothes. . . . I'm strictly a song-and-dance girl. I can act enough to get by. Let's face it, that's the limit of my talents. If I have a good enough director he can usually pull me through the tight places. But I feel more secure if they let me do a few numbers. I'm no Bette Davis . . . If I play Sophie my fans will expect me to arise from the ocean with seaweed in my hair and sing something."

Costume designer Orry-Kelly found working with Grable a nightmare at this time. Charles LeMaire had brought him in to create the new, toned-down Grable look in *Miss Pilgrim*. Now he was persuaded to do her clothes in *Mother Wore Tights,* another turn-of-the-century musical comedy. Still smarting from the negative fan mail about the look Orry-Kelly had fashioned for her in *Miss Pilgrim,* Grable insisted on showing as much leg as possible. She fought with Orry-Kelly over every costume. He retaliated with charges that her choices were totally inconsistent with the styles of the period. LeMaire, who supervised the costuming, sardonically recalled: "The Madam insisted upon pastel pumps, nude hose, and mid-calf skirts—with slits. She often looked completely modern with the exception of her lowered hems." Orry-Kelly refused ever to work with her again, even despite the box-office success of the film that proved Betty's instincts on how the public expected her to look.

Grable begged Zanuck to use Fred Astaire as her costar. An astute idea, obviously, but for reasons known only to Darryl F.

Zanuck, he refused. Betty would call this her worst professional disappointment. Astaire, under contract to MGM, may have been too valuable a property to loan out. Zanuck may also have balked at MGM's asking price. But the likelier reason is that Zanuck felt Grable's brassiness would clash with Astaire's gentlemanly elegance. Zanuck usually pitted her against macho types like George Montgomery, Victor Mature, Dale Robertson, MacDonald Carey, and Douglas Fairbanks, Jr.

Betty next insisted on James Cagney, an excellent choice. But Cagney, still riding a crest of popularity for his Academy Award–winning performance as George M. Cohan in *Yankee Doodle Dandy,* was fetching enormous fees. Warner Bros., owner of Cagney's contract and an old Fox rival, asked an impossible sum for his services.

Zanuck then introduced Grable to Dan Dailey, who was to become her favorite costar. An ex–Broadway hoofer, Dailey had appeared in desultory film musicals and mediocre melodramas. He badly needed a break. Fortunately for him, Betty took to Dailey immediately; on the strength of her approval he was hired. It was to him—and not to Marilyn Monroe, as frequently reported—that Betty said: "I've got mine—now you get yours." Unlike most stars, Betty was ever-willing to share the spotlight. *Mother Wore Tights* made Dailey a star. It also represented a triumph for Betty, whose fans stormed the box office and made *Tights* the hit of the year and its song "Kokomo, Indiana" a sensation.

The plot bore uncanny parallels to Betty's personal life. She and Dailey played a touring husband-and-wife vaudevillian team who often left their two daughters in the care of their grandmother. Torn between family and career, the tormented heroine is advised by her mother, angel-faced Sara Allgood, to concentrate on her career and leave the girls at home—even at the risk of losing their love. When the girls grow older, they are sent away to expensive private schools. The oldest, Mona Freeman, rejects her parents and admits she's ashamed of their show-business life.

Betty turned in an affecting performance and found an ingenious way to expose her legs. In an early scene she auditions for a show, and the producer (William Frawley, later of *I Love Lucy)* asks her to raise her floor-length skirt, a common practice in vaudeville days. Millions of fans in movie theaters throughout America beheld the legendary wartime pin-up in a moment of nostalgic déjà vu. America still adored Betty Grable.

In this film Betty's rare attention to detail and in-depth characterization reflected her off-screen emotional involvement with Dan Dailey. She had fallen in love with him. In view of his homosexuality, their affair has to rate as one of Hollywood's strangest. His confused sexuality and despondent nature evoked in Betty her most maternal and protective instincts—qualities that, ironically, she held in very short supply for her own daughters.

Born in New York City in 1915, Dailey was one of four children. His father, who changed his name from O'Dailey to Dailey, was a hotel man. He strongly disapproved of theatrical people because they often disappeared from his establishment before paying the bill.

Overriding his father's protests, Dailey and his sister, Irene, who would later in life achieve Broadway's highest accolades in *The Subject Was Roses,* managed to get into show business. Dan was already a talented hoofer at age six. He once explained, "A hoofer is different from a dancer. A hoofer is strictly a rhythm man. Everything he does springs primarily from rhythm—he thinks in figures and designs. When I hear music I start moving around and the dance develops inevitably from the rhythm of the music. Dancers do the movements and *then* put the sound to it."

Lorenz Hart first spotted Dailey in a vaudeville review and cast him in two collaborations with Richard Rodgers, *Babes in Arms* and *I Married an Angel.* Those performances attracted MGM's attention and Dailey was given a contract.

After twenty flops at MGM, all nonmusical, Dailey married Los Angeles socialite Elizabeth Hotert in 1942. He joined the Army, serving as a lieutenant and then captain with the Ninety-ninth Infantry Division in Italy. In a fight with another soldier, he sustained a permanent injury to the roof of his mouth; a steel plate had to be implanted.

After viewing the first rushes of *Mother Wore Tights,* Zanuck shrewdly negotiated to purchase Dan Dailey's contract from MGM. The year 1946 marked not only the beginning of Dailey's successful film career but also the birth of his first child, a son.

At thirty-one, full of boyish charm and sunny exuberance, Dailey enraptured Hollywood gorgons Hedda Hopper and Louella Parsons. "Dan Dailey," Hopper gushed, "as the new curly-headed wonder child, has asked for nothing, griped about nothing, and has flashed no more temperament than a turtle." Not to be outdone by her razor-tongued rival, Louella Parsons simpered, "He's a thoroughly *nice boy,* sincere in his work and happy at his home." Though Betty definitely preferred sexually aggressive and assertive men, she found great pleasure in nurturing Dailey's neuroses, which served as "escape" from the many pressures of the studio and her dismal home life. Dailey, who genuinely adored his son and enjoyed his home life, continued to wear women's clothing while at home and sometimes even in public.

*Confidential* magazine published photographs of Dailey in drag. In the scandal that followed, Betty Grable stood behind him. Thanks in part to his enormous popularity within the industry, Dailey's career survived. It is also possible the studio simply had too much money invested in him to drop him. According to Charles LeMaire, Dailey had a penchant for Linda Darnell's gowns. LeMaire had to warn a designer that Dailey was making midnight raids on the wardrobe department. Demonstrating an unusual broad-mindedness for the uptight 1940s, Betty urged Dailey to embrace his latent homosexuality and enjoy gay sex. She fixed him up with young gay actors who regularly sought her out.

However bizarre it was, the affair with Dailey offered Betty relief from a home life that careened totally out of control. "My parents were never together," their daughter Jessie would recall years later. "He did his thing and she did hers. I don't know, but it was just like two different people—we just didn't do things together as a family."

Though the Jameses happily posed together at the dinner table for photographers, they rarely shared a meal together.

The occasions when they did were fraught with the tension of imminent violence. Betty accused Harry of being weak, "a faggot," a miserable failure as a responsible family man. Harry seldom argued back. But once, Jessie recalled, he picked up a juicer from the kitchen counter and threw it at Betty, who watched in horror as it whizzed by her and crashed on the floor.

Both Betty and Harry were on the verge of getting into serious trouble with their gambling. Betty could afford the vice. Harry couldn't, but that did not deter him from appropriating her earnings for use at the racetrack at Del Mar near San Diego.

Ollie Hughes, a Grable intimate who worked in the wardrobe department throughout the years at Fox, said Harry abused Betty on the lot and gambled away her fortune. "He spent it," Hughes said. "Harry got away with all that. I tell you I didn't like James because of the way he treated Betty. But she'd never say anything against him. And he spent all the money. I imagine he spent more than three million dollars of hers. She lost the big ranch she had, and everything. He got into horse racing and gambling. And that's what killed her."

James's interest in racehorses and betting started long before he married Betty. A friend who had grown tired of Harry's relentless questioning about horses and horse racing offered him a half interest in a horse—and from then on he was hooked. By the time he married Betty he already owned a small stable of horses. In 1947 the Jameses became partners in a $125,000 string of horses under the ownership banner of the Betty J Stables, managed by Betty's father, Conn.

Before Dan Dailey came along, Betty Grable tried to escape her problems at home in other dalliances at the studio, where her private dressing room offered a convenient pied-à-terre. Over a round of drinks with band singer Helen Forrest and writer Alvin Marill, Dick Haymes admitted that he had a "rough go" with Harry James, putting an end to their close friendship. Haymes costarred with Betty in *Billy Rose's Diamond Horseshoe* and *The Shocking Miss Pilgrim;* eventually he and Betty had an affair. When Harry James found out, he came after Dick

Haymes with a gun and threatened to kill him if Haymes "ever laid hands on her again."

One day Betty and Dan Dailey were locked in her dressing room when Harry made an unexpected visit to Fox. His suspicions were aroused when studio personnel, attempting to cover for Betty, told him she had gone home to check up on Jessica, who was then only a few months old. Angered by the obvious cover-up, Harry broke into her dressing room, where he found them together. Harry began to beat Betty. She scrambled for the door and finally managed to escape. Advised by the studio to go home to attend to her bruises, she left in utter humiliation. For two months Betty refused to speak to Harry when he put in an appearance at home. In time he would batter her again, and invariably, after a period of sullen anger, she would say she loved Harry and "no other man."

Betty made the cover of *Time* magazine on August 23, 1948. The qualities that had put her there—she was pert, sassy, and blonde, and all America loved her—were beginning to seem a bit jejune. In the postwar period the big Fox hits were films of high social import such as *Pinky, Gentleman's Agreement,* and *The Snake Pit*. Fox accordingly insisted she forgo the backstage musicals audiences had come to expect from her, and against her better judgment she agreed to star in Ernst Lubitsch's *That Lady in Ermine,* based on the operetta *This Is the Moment*. Betty played a girl who steps barefoot out of a portrait in search of the perfect man, played by Douglas Fairbanks, Jr. She wore a highly publicized costume made from 900 ermine skins. Many believed Lubitsch's sophisticated European touch would help create a softer and even whimsical Grable. Instead, the German-born director diabolically exploited her all-American, down-to-earth appeal to present his satirical view of U.S. social attitudes.

After eight days of filming, Lubitsch, a veteran of four coronaries, died suddenly, in the midst of his fifth. He was replaced by another foreign-born director, Otto Preminger, whose heavy-handed style failed to sustain Lubitsch's vision as established in the scenes shot earlier. As a result, an uneven film teetered on the brink of silliness.

During the filming, body-makeup artist Bunny Gardell pointed out to a Fox publicist, Sonia Wolfson, that Grable's feet were exceptionally beautiful. "Though lots of girls have pretty legs," Wolfson said, "few, if any, have truly beautiful feet." She contacted the California Chiropodists Association, who just a year before had named Grable's rival, June Haver, as "the star with the most beautiful feet." Three chiropodists converged on Grable's dressing room to see for themselves. After their inspection, they unanimously agreed Betty did indeed have remarkable feet. Studio photographers were quickly ushered in. Grable, barefoot, posed with the three doctors as they held her feet on bended knee. "Flawless," Wolfson said. "No bent toes, no corns, no calluses."

Though *That Lady in Ermine* was poorly reviewed, Betty was still regarded as an institution and *Time* chose this occasion to canonize the pin-up girl with a four-page cover story. When interviewed, Billie took the opportunity to gloat: "They said Betty wouldn't ever get anywhere in the movies." The reviewer wrote, "Betty and her square-jawed artlessness fits *[sic]* badly into an atmosphere of languorous waltzes and yearning tziganes and dark uncontrollable passion . . . The nice-kid-after-all formula is what the public loves, and that isn't what it gets."

Extremely disappointed with the film, Zanuck cringed when he heard her common-showgirl readings in the fabled historical setting. As far as Zanuck was concerned, Betty Grable was finished. All that remained was to find ways to force her out of Fox. Like carrion crows, other Fox executives taunted Grable, saying, "You're only as good as your last film, kid," and virtually invited the press to do her in. Certainly Betty could no longer count on the publicity department for protection. After being named the "Most Uncooperative Actress of 1948" (she tied with Ingrid Bergman), Betty blasted: "When I was at Paramount I was getting absolutely no parts in pictures, but I was queen of the publicity department. I worked ten hours a day, posing for every still anybody could dream up. They even pushed me inside a cage with a tiger once—with cameramen hidden behind every bar . . . I was always in a bathing suit. That's when all this 'legs Grable' stuff started. So now—I'm uncooperative. They get me for publicity when they catch me!"

Open warfare had begun.

And yet Betty's personal reviews for the movie, in retrospect, are not damning. "Frankly," wrote Bosley Crowther, "she isn't as agile with the wit and glance as she might be, but she sings with the gusto of a lady who understands the meaning of a song . . ."

In 1947, for the sixth consecutive year, Betty Grable made the list of the top ten box-office stars. Fox's haste to kill off the queen bee seems curious. They would not find it an easy task. She held an iron-clad contract.

Grable belonged to the war years. Now World War II and everything associated with it were rejected by an unsentimental public. Perhaps it was symbolic that a museum asked Grable for a cast of her legs. Fox's head makeup man, Ben Nye, accommodated. Grable's legs went on display. They were now a part of history.

# CHAPTER 10

"My mother had a perverted, puritan view of sex," Jessica "Jessie" James Yahner recalls, reflecting on the bittersweet memories she still holds for her mother, Betty Grable. Sex was never to be referred to in any way, Jessie discovered early in life. While walking with her mother and friends in Beverly Hills, Jessie, still a small child, giggled as she pointed in the direction of a woman in an advanced state of pregnancy. Betty whirled and struck her in the mouth with the back of her hand. Humiliated and in pain, Jessie was forced to stand at rigid attention as Betty unleashed a torrent of obscenities that stopped traffic.

Speaking softly and guardedly about her turbulent years as the youngest daughter of two of the most popular entertainers in show business, Jessica said, "My parents didn't live a Hollywood life. Sometimes I feel I missed out on something, especially when I'd talk to other kids and they'd say, 'Oh, we entertained so and so.' She wanted us to have a 'normal' childhood."

Jessie grew up in the luxury of the Jameses' Beverly Hills home, sealed off from the world and attended to by a stiffly regimented team of governesses, gardeners, housekeepers, and cooks. One cook referred to those years in the James household as "pure living hell."

At home, Betty Grable was a domineering tyrant, barking out orders and demanding the kind of slavish submission usually reserved for royalty. She took her household duties seriously—too seriously. Despite the full staff of servants, Betty shopped for food and did the family washing, drying, and ironing. Charles LeMaire said Betty would cart her family's laundry to the studio, where she washed and ironed between takes. During the filming of a laundry scene in *The Farmer Takes a Wife,* Betty, under pressure over a contractual dispute that led to a suspension, brazenly carried her dirty laundry to the set. She washed it in front of the rolling camera.

Marjorie described one of her infrequent visits to the James home: "I dropped by one Sunday afternoon and instead of resting I found my sister ironing. I wouldn't be doing any of that with all the hired help she had."

The staff was usually rattled by Betty's shrieked commands. A former governess said, "She always screamed at us—and she was never ever satisfied with the amount of work we did." The more courageous openly defied her—and were promptly fired. "Mrs. James," said one black maid, fed up with daily harassment, "when I die I hope I come back as one of your dogs." The household changing of the guard became a monthly ritual.

Betty felt threatened by even the most casual or superficial criticism or question put before her by *anyone,* household staff, studio subordinates, and daughters included. Unable to distinguish feelings of insecurity from feelings of constant fear, Betty seized upon the only two emotions she could get in touch with: anger and rage.

"Who knows," Jessie comments, "for all of her strength, it was just a show. But you really should have seen what she did to our help. She treated them the same way she treated me—the same way she treated my sister."

When Vicki was four and Jessie one, Betty, in admitting to

Hedda Hopper that she often fired her children's nurses, revealed a disturbing paranoia. Speaking of one nurse, Betty said, "She was a wonderful nurse, but she took over Vicki completely. Became too attached to her, indulged her, and I had a feeling I was intruding anytime I wanted to care for my baby. Maybe that's what she thought I wanted, being an actress. Well, it *wasn't!* For one thing, I wasn't going to let anyone else have the fun of raising her, *winning her affection.* I realized what was going on so I fired her."

As a child Vicki once tried to emulate her father by playing the trumpet as her mother sat pensively nearby. Betty once told a newspaper reporter, "She has a terrific crush on her father. She developed a big yen to play the trumpet like her father, but I talked her out of that. When she gets older I'll let her study the piano—if she wants to for her pleasure only, and not with any idea of a career. Harry and I will let them decide." Jessie ruefully recalls: "My mother wouldn't do that. She wouldn't give us any musical lessons. But I wish she had. And I always wanted to sing with my dad's band. To me that would have been just great!" Given the enriched musical backgrounds of which she and Harry were keepers, it was extraordinary of Betty to deny music to her children. Since she was never permitted to share the love Harry showered on his trumpet, neither would her daughter.

When Vicki attended horse races with her parents, Harry would give her some money to bet on horses of her own choosing. If the horse failed even to place, Vicki, unable to control her anger, stormed out of the turf box where her parents were sitting. "There she goes," Harry said, "acting just like her mother."

Betty earned yet another title in Hollywood—"Queen of the Handicappers." Even the most jaded bookies and gamblers were amazed at her ability to retain trivial facts about the hundreds of horses she handicapped. Grable could scan a racing form in seconds, then knowledgeably discuss the merits and shortcomings of each horse. Whenever unfortunate fans approached her at the racetrack, she abruptly cut them off with a stony silence; her game was not to be interrupted.

Betty met her closest friend, Betty Ritz, at the Del Mar

racetrack. Ritz, who was married to Harry Ritz, a member of the very popular comedy team the Ritz Brothers, recalls: "We went out, four of us. We were Betty and Harry and Betty and Harry [Ritz]. We were having dinner, and we went to the ladies' room and I asked if I could use her comb. I looked at this big, long, one-foot comb with narrow teeth at one end and big teeth at the other. In the complete comb there might have been ten teeth. I figured she was joking with me, but I went ahead and kind of raked it through my hair. The comb snapped in half and Betty just about had hysterics. 'You've broken my comb! That is the worst omen in the world. You've ruined my luck for the whole season.' The next morning I went to a drugstore and bought every comb in sight. I had them all gift-wrapped in a big cigar box with beautiful big bows on it, went to the races, and put it down on their table at the Turf Club with a note inside: 'I hope that this will change your luck. We can be friends and have a lot of fun with all the combs.' Betty unwrapped that package when she came in and looked at me and just got hysterical laughing. She came running up to me and said, 'You're a gal I'm gonna like. You've got a great sense of humor.'"

Betty was comfortable in the world of horse racing and gambling. She loved the personalities who were drawn to the casinos of Las Vegas and Reno. She would often drive to Tijuana to spend her days away from the studio blissfully at the dog races and horse races, unobserved. Later she would go barhopping with jockeys and their wives or mistresses. At both the Hollywood Park and Del Mar racetracks, Betty always maintained her own turf box where she entertained horse-racing promoters, gangsters, horse owners, gamblers, and jockeys like Willie Shoemaker, Henry Moreno, and scores of others.

Every year, for six weeks beginning in September, the Jameses suspended busy work schedules and flocked down to Del Mar with their daughters. There they would gamble, soak up the sun, swim, golf, and hike in the nearby Torrey Pines. These blissful respites were the only times the four spent together as a family. "Horses are our mutual interest, so the races are our opportunity," Betty told Hedda Hopper.

Bing Crosby, major stockholder of the Del Mar racetrack and president of the multimillion dollar enterprise, drew a score of Hollywood greats to the track—Darryl Zanuck, Louis B. Mayer, Harry Warren, Spencer Tracy, Barbara Stanwyck, Robert Taylor, George Raft, Errol Flynn, and Don Ameche were among the visitors. The thrill of gambling, not the love of horses, lured them to the tracks, where some spent much of their fortunes. When Betty and Harry's horse Kab won a $100,000 purse for them, Betty declared that winning an Oscar could never equal the joy of winning a race.

During the filming of *When My Baby Smiles at Me,* director Walter Lang, fifty musicians, and three times as many chorus people, dancers, and extras were dressed and waiting for La Grable one morning, when she received a telegram in her dressing room. She summoned her gambling pal Bill Smith. "Read this," she said, handing him the telegram. "Go over and tell Eddie to bet for me." As Bill Smith would later explain, "There was a bookie named Eddie on the lot who hung around the casting office. He was there primarily for Betty—she bet big, you see." Smith took her $1,000 to the casting office for Eddie, but Eddie, only minutes before, had been kicked off the lot by the new unit manager. "It was around ten forty-five in the morning and the set was completely set to shoot," Smith said. "It cost seventy-five thousand to a hundred thousand dollars to shoot this thing. So I went back to Betty's dressing room where she was being made up."

"Betty, no bet," Smith told her.

"Whatdya mean, no bet?"

"They just threw Eddie off the lot."

Betty threw her costume on the floor, put on her dress, and walked off the lot. When Zanuck, a heavy gambler himself, learned his star had walked out, he summoned Smith to his office.

"God damn it," he shouted, "what happened to Grable?"

"Somebody threw her bookie off the lot, Darryl."

"Who threw him off the lot?" Zanuck reached for the phone to begin an investigation. Smith was ordered to get Grable and bring her back.

It was 1:30 P.M. when Smith knocked on Betty's door at home. "Tell Zanuck I wasn't at home," she shouted, "and you—you get the hell out of here." Later that afternoon, she phoned Smith and asked him to tell Zanuck she would be back on the set the following morning. Smith added, "The horse, by the way, didn't even place."

# CHAPTER 11

"Musicians represent no commitment," Harry James's daughter Jessica comments. "My father was very shy. His music—that's how he expressed how he felt, and even though he wasn't at home much, he'd always come back to change his shoes." Her father admitted to Jessica that it took him an inordinate amount of courage to speak to his audiences—even a simple "Hello, folks." Two fifths of vodka each day fortified him.

"It's almost impossible to go out someplace after working eight shows in six days," he said. "When you get a day off you just feel like staying home. Or occasionally, like on a Sunday, if we have a night away from the show, we'll play a one-night stand with just the band, where we really get to stretch out, so we don't go crazy."

Harry loved baseball. Hedda Hopper wrote, "Harry James with his orchestra ballplayers at the La Cienega Park last Saturday slid into third base and he twisted his right foot from under him and broke a bone. The foot has now been put in a cast."

Betty, proud of her husband's passion for the great American pastime, boasted, "The nicest thing of all is the absolutely amazing way our hobbies and interests line up. For instance, Harry's wild about baseball. On his tours he'll stop over anywhere they'll let him play in a game. Good heavens—I was raised in St. Louis with baseball all around me. There's never been any other game in my life. When I was a kid, the St. Louis Cardinals stayed here [the Forest Park Hotel] and Rogers Hornsby used to toss me up to the ceiling every now and then and my mother used to coax me with pony rides to take my dancing lessons."

The Jameses' enslavement to gambling was not limited to the racetracks of Los Angeles. They also frequented Las Vegas casinos, where together they disposed of fortunes. Betty often joined Harry for a long weekend in Vegas, where he played regularly. One weekend they arranged to stay with Betty and Harry Ritz at the Flamingo Hotel, where Ritz was appearing with his brothers.

Betty Ritz picked them up at the airport and brought them to the hotel only long enough to drop off their luggage. Then the two Bettys and two Harrys headed for the casino until it was time for the dinner show. Immediately afterward it was back to the crap tables.

"At one time Betty Grable was losing seventy-five thousand dollars," Betty Ritz remembered. "I know Harry James was losing over a hundred thousand dollars. And then we got it back down, at about six o'clock in the morning, to where he was losing sixty, she was losing maybe forty . . . We slept for about three hours and then we went over to the place where they had horse racing. You could bet all the horse races, all around the country. We started betting on the horses and I don't know how much they won or lost. They left with Betty losing twenty-five thousand and Harry thirty-five thousand."

The gambling fever that gripped Betty and Harry throughout their lives wiped out any business sense they might have brought to bear on their huge earnings. They rarely conducted their business with reputable advisors, moreover, choosing instead to wheel and deal with other gambling types. Betty was linked socially with Al Capone and his family. The Capones adored Grable and offered her the run of their Florida Bay estate, complete with household staff and chauffeur.

The Jameses' lack of business acumen may have been the result of the harsh economic times in which they grew up. Born in the seesaw post–World War I economy, Betty and Harry had both been personally affected by the Depression by age twelve. Harry's parents regularly risked everything—careers, meager savings, and even their lives for the thrills and excitement of a gypsy circus life. The senior Grables, too, speculated dangerously with their personal happiness and careers. Bud blew his family's savings on a highly volatile commodities stock exchange. Billie, on the remote chance of making Betty a star, threw away whatever love and security she had by abandoning husband and daughter.

Betty's inclination to take risks had set in long before she thought about gambling in Las Vegas. Even now, with her luck running out in Hollywood, Betty looked to Las Vegas, where the odds for another kind of success might still be in her favor.

Although once named Mother of the Year, parenting was not one of Betty Grable's gifts. One night she returned home late from an exacting day at the studio, long after the girls had been sent off to bed. As she entered her bedroom, the silence of the sleeping household was suddenly broken by Jessie's piercing cries.

Betty rushed to her five-year-old to comfort her. Jessie explained that her nanny, who had taken such good care of her and loved her, had deserted her. Unaware the nanny had been fired, Jessie asked, "Won't you go out to find her and bring her back because I miss her and need someone to take care of me?"

Grable pushed her daughter away and flew into a rage, cruelly taunting Jessie and daring her to leave their home with "this nurse you love so much." Jessie fled the room, Betty on her heels, screaming and cursing. She seized the terrified child, pushed her down, and began to pull on her hair and strike her.

Betty frequently summoned Vicki and Jessie to her bedroom at night; Betty was afraid of sleeping alone in a dark room. By morning, when the effects of her increasing alcohol consumption had worn off, the two girls crawled out of bed, frightened of disturbing her. They knew waking their mother from a deep sleep would provoke a barrage of threats.

"Don't ever speak to me before I've had my first morning cup of coffee," Grable used to warn her daughters.

"Wow!" Jessie said years later, shaking her head in painful recollection. "You bet—you just didn't wake her up. She was nasty."

Betty Ritz commented, "You wouldn't dare talk to her until she'd finished her crossword puzzle—for only then would she talk to you."

Though Betty would lash out with a stream of four-letter words in front of her daughters, she expected them not to follow her own example. "Don't ever, *ever* use a word of profanity," she commanded, enforcing her double standard with swift stinging slaps across the mouth whenever they violated the law. She would curse even as she administered punishment for cursing.

It weighed heavily on Betty that her lifelong dream of a happy home and family was never to be. There was no one to lean on—except Billie. As Betty once said, "Every girl in the world wants to find the right man. Someone who is sympathetic and understanding and helpful and strong . . ."

Betty was afraid of sleeping alone because of a problem that had plagued her since childhood. "In St. Louis I developed the aggravating habit of sleepwalking," she said. "Even now I have to be constantly watchful at night and my windows must be opened from the top . . . I'd still like to know of a cure." Though somnambulism is not considered unusual for children during their "growing pains" period, it is diagnosed as very serious when it persists through adulthood, as it did in Betty's case.

Marjorie recalled that Billie, trying not to wake Betty during her frequent sleepwalking trances, would say, "Betty, go to bed," and the sleeping Betty would obey. Once Betty was staying on the thirty-seventh floor of New York's Waldorf-Astoria; terrified of heights, she phoned the front desk and asked that a bellboy be sent up with a hammer and nails. When he arrived Betty instructed him to nail the windows shut.

"Miss Grable, no one can get into your room on the thirty-seventh floor," he protested.

"I'm not worried about them getting in," she said. "It's *me* getting out that I'm worried about."

On the success of *Mother Wore Tights,* Fox shoved Grable back into her formula musicals. She managed to regain some of her old studio clout. *When My Baby Smiles at Me* was based on the twenties play *Burlesque,* which had been filmed in 1929 as *The Dance of Life* and in 1937 as *Swing High, Swing Low,* starring Carole Lombard and Fred MacMurray. Grable's version updated the story to the 1940s.

Betty managed more than her usual cardboard characterization, perhaps because she was working again with her beloved Dan Dailey. *When My Baby* was a typical Grable vehicle—the backstage story of a married vaudeville team forced to cope with *his* alcoholism and declining popularity as *her* career simultaneously begins to flourish.

With the exception of her sensitive, touching interpretation of the blues ballad "By the Way," Betty appeared preoccupied. In many scenes she appeared to be giving the film to Dailey.

Robert Wagner, then a young stargazer who later joined Fox's roster of junior players, often witnessed Grable's tough-star temperament. But he later defended his friend: "When you're carrying that many people, and I know the weight of that—you're the number-one star of the business! Your pictures are the highest and brightest box office in the country. You're the highest-paid woman in the world . . . There's a lot of people to contend with along the line and it's a gigantic responsibility. And I can tell you one thing. The studio made a lot of money from her, and when she was on top she was a very protected investment and one they kept working all the time."

Wagner believes Grable had the potential to be a serious actress, a potential she could not recognize. He calls her "a true and highly disciplined professional. When all that brassy exterior was stripped away, you could get close to her—to see that fun-loving and generous side of her. If she could have exposed that side, it would have been wonderful. But there was no chance of it. She may not have allowed it, but then she also didn't have a chance to exercise it because she was established as a number-one musical pin-up. How the hell could she get out of that?"

Though Wagner was aware of her battles on the lot, he saw only the gambler side of Grable. "Grable was a pretty good handicapper and I can remember a couple of times when she got so angry with the studio she stormed off the lot and headed for the nearest racetrack."

"A girl like Grable who's been carrying the box office for seven straight years ought to have some very special recognition," director Henry Koster said, but Fox was again convinced Betty's name above the title no longer guaranteed box-office receipts. Her brand of musical films had been abandoned by the public, and the advent of a new film color process, De Luxe, superseded the luscious Technicolor so complimentary to Betty. Technicolor's pink, lavender, and purple incandescence had become a Grable trademark. Now De Luxe made the old Grable musicals look like garish cartoons.

Yet American movie-theater exhibitors still named Betty to the top ten elite. Told she had made it again, Grable murmured, "It's a funny thing—I haven't a shrewd bone in me. I had no investments. I never wanted to be anything or to possess anything. When I started working I thought I could not have a career and marriage too. I am just a lucky girl."

Her former lover Victor Mature, then establishing himself as a superstar of biblical beefcake extravaganzas, costarred with Betty in *Wabash Avenue*, a remake of her earlier hit, *Coney Island*. Betty became one of the few major stars to dare to remake one of her own pictures—and do it successfully.

Happily, the Grable pin-up figure still looked great. Of the opening number, "Shimmy Like My Sister Kate," Bosley Crowther wrote: "This round and voluptuous young lady proceeds to unlimber herself in a manner her sister, we feel, could not surpass. And this form of agitation rather sets the style for the whole show. They never get above the level of the shimmy in *Wabash Avenue.*"

In 1951, Betty starred again with Dan Dailey in the dismal *Call Me Mister*, based on the Broadway smash. Dailey was beset by serious problems; along with alcoholism, he was coping with mental depression that would become life-threatening. By the end of that year, after divorcing his wife, and after several drunk-driving charges were featured in the nation's press, Dailey entered the Menninger psychiatric center in Kansas for six months.

"I'd cracked," Dailey said. "Some people can face the rough spots in their lives and get through them, but I was in pieces." During his six-month stay at the Menninger hospital, Dailey studied painting and sculpture as part of his therapy and sent some of his works to Betty. "You don't know the satisfaction you can get from just chopping wood," he wrote to her. "You stand back and look and say, 'I did that!'"

After *Call Me Mister* died at the box office, Betty finally admitted, in private, her film career was ebbing. She no longer depended solely on her Hollywood earnings, taking her theater and nightclub acts across the country, parading a coy, simplistic, peek-a-boo showgirl routine. Grable clung to her old-fashioned hairdo, ignoring the fashionable skull-hugging Shirley Temple poodle cut. She rejected even the studio hairstylist who tried to soften her "butch" style. The studio received thousands of letters from fans criticizing Grable's hairdo. Zanuck ordered her to change it. But Betty dug in her heels. Sidney Skolsky wrote, "She's famous for the *upswept* hairdo she introduced to her pictures but offscreen she never wears it that way." Off screen, Grable's hair, after years of studio bleaching and machine drying, had begun to thin and turn kinky. She took to wearing wigs, false hairpieces, and bandannas.

Soon she was talking of retirement: "A lot of people say you go crazy without work. Not me. I'd stay at home with the kids. I'd go with Harry once in a while when he's on the road. I'm sure it will all be over in a heap when it happens."

Home with the kids was a scene out of Grand Guignol. "It would happen at all different times," Jessie remembered. "She'd come in when I'd be dressing for school in the morning and she'd just tear me apart physically. Grab me, pull my hair, slap me and push me down. It used to take me half an hour to go up to her and ask her if I could go across the street to visit my girlfriend. To go anywhere we had to screw up the courage."

And where was Harry?

"Well, once when we were home and I had done something bad in the kitchen, my mother took the cigarette in her hand and she turned and grabbed me as she twisted the cigarette into my arm. I started screaming at the top of my lungs and my dad, who was outside, comes running in and he asks, 'What's going on in here?'" Looking to him for protection, Jessie screamed again, "Look what she did to me." Jessie stretched her arm out before him, displaying an ugly burn.

Harry James "shook his head, turned around and walked right out. I guess," Jessie added protectively, "he just couldn't deal with it."

Betty dances her heart out in *Down Argentine Way.* Alice Faye had been originally intended for the role, but she cancelled out. A new Fox queen assumed her reign.
*Courtesy The Bettmann Archive 20th Century–Fox.*

• • •

Betty on the arm of her lover, George Raft, at the premiere of her dramatic debut in *A Yank in the R.A.F.*
*Courtesy The Bettmann Archive.*

• • •

Betty Grable, Victor Mature, and Carole Landis.
*Courtesy The Bettmann Archive 20th Century–Fox.*

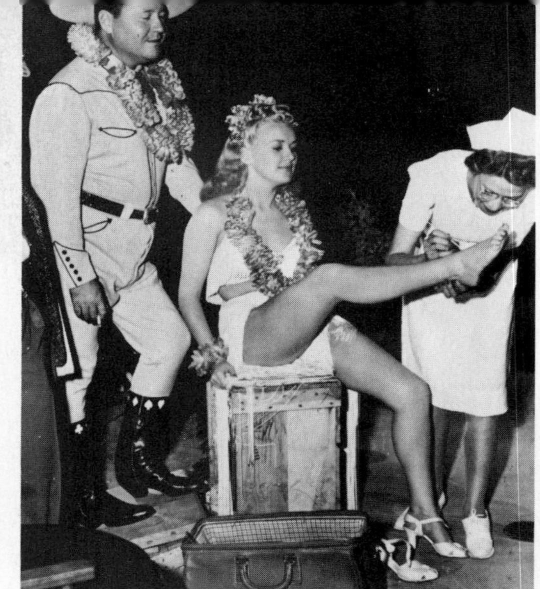

Once voted as having the prettiest pair of feet ever, Betty has them attended to on the set of *Song of the Islands* while costar Jack Oakie looks admiringly on.
*Courtesy The Bettmann Archive*
*20th Century–Fox.*

• • •

Betty clowns on the set with Victor Mature during the filming of *Song of the Islands.*
*Courtesy The Bettmann Archive*
*20th Century–Fox.*

• • •

The favorite pin-up girl for GIs the world over introduces the "identification anklet." Hers was a gift from George Raft.
*Courtesy The Bettmann Archive.*

Betty and Phil Silvers in 1942.
*Photo The Museum of Modern Art Film Stills Archives.*

• • •

Frequent Grable costar John Payne, Betty, and George Raft at the Academy Awards in 1942.
*Photo The Museum of Modern Art Film Stills Archives.*

• • •

Renee Hubert adjusts Betty's gown as Marie Brasselle and Leon Shamroy observe preparations on the set. Betty was well-known for her tyrannical treatment of costume designers and their staff.
*Photo The Museum of Modern Art Film Stills Archives 20th Century–Fox.*

*(Left)*
Betty and Harry James honeymooning in 1943—America's perfect couple.
*Photo The Museum of Modern Art Film Stills Archives.*

• • •

*(Right)*
Harry teaches Betty pieces of a new arrangement in their Beverly Hills home. Betty wanted to record the songs she made famous in her movies, but Darryl Zanuck wouldn't let her. Under an assumed name she recorded a hit with Harry in the late forties, "I Can't Begin to Tell You."
*Courtesy The Bettmann Archive.*

• • •

*(Bottom)*
In 1943, at the peak of her career, Betty Grable added her name, and a leg, to the names of celebrities inscribed in immortality outside Sid Grauman's Chinese Theatre.

Master Sergeant Bert Strickland, technical advisor of the military numbers in *Pin-Up Girl,* displays his favorite view of Betty's legs.
*Photo The Museum of Modern Art Film Stills Archives.*

• • •

A tired couple at their ranch retreat.
*Photo The Museum of Modern Art Film Stills Archives.*

Betty and Martha Raye in *Pin-Up Girl*. Betty plays Lorry Jones, queen of the USO clubhouse in Missoula, Montana. Lorry sends out pin-ups of herself autographed with "scads of love" to servicemen friends.
*Photo The Museum of Modern Art Film Stills Archives 20th Century–Fox.*

• • • • •

Betty and costar John Payne sneak an affectionate behind-the-scenes hug during filming of *The Dolly Sisters*. Can you identify the man in the picture on Grable's dressing table?
*Photo The Museum of Modern Art Film Stills Archives 20th Century–Fox.*

Betty poses with newborn daughter Jessica. Jessie's sister, Vicky, the "pin-up" baby, is three years her elder.
*Courtesy The Bettmann Archive.*

• • •

Betty's Beverly Hills home.
*Photo The Museum of Modern Art Film Stills Archives.*

# CHAPTER 12

*Meet Me After the Show* was another disappointment for Fox. Critics ignored Betty's dancing, the best she had done in years. Cruelly, they focused on her spreading figure and deepening wrinkles.

Travilla was now designing her costumes and discovering—like every designer before him—she was virtually impossible to work with. "She was an aging pretty little girl who was showing some mileage and it was hurting," Travilla said.

Grable's pot belly was difficult to conceal in the revealing costumes her audience expected her to wear, though Travilla believed she looked better without any clothes on. Short-waisted and long-legged, Betty's figure did not reflect the ideal look of the fifties. And the advent of CinemaScope made costuming Betty even more of a headache. "I thought of her as probably one of the rudest women I had ever met," Travilla said. "She treated me as if I didn't know my business. One day I made the fatal mistake of walking out into the hallway from my office during a fitting. When I came back my outer door was locked. I stood outside and knocked on the door and heard Betty say, 'We're not ready yet'—and then I waited forty-five minutes.

"'Well, you might as well come in now,' she said. 'It's a mess.' I went in and the dress had been totally pulled apart. The sleeves were out, the neckline had been pulled out and pinned differently—all kinds of alterations. There was nothing you could do with it. I was frightened of her, not having worked before with an abusive star as I found her to be. So then I apologized and said, 'If I could have seen it before you—'

"'There was no way,' she interrupted. 'It was awful.' And so that's how that movie went. It never seemed to get better."

At the start of the filming, director Richard Sale went to Betty's dressing room to wish her luck. He knocked and said, "Good morning, Miss Grable."

"Good morning," she snapped, opening the door. "Is that all you have to say, because I'm busy."

"I'm sorry," the startled director said, turning away.

When Charles LeMaire complained to Travilla about the rising cost of an unfinished costume, Travilla said, "If we could only find where the crotch is, we'd finish the costume," referring to Betty's chronic complaints about the crotch pinching her whenever she moved. Travilla swore he'd never work with her again.

Despite these tantrums, a rolling camera made Betty perk up, pull in her pot belly, and transform herself into a twenty-five-year-old woman.

Upon the completion of *Meet Me After the Show* in 1951, Hollywood reeled with the announcement that Betty Grable had been formally suspended by Fox for refusing to appear in *The Girl Next Door*. Her part went to June Haver. "And though never officially discussed," one reporter wrote, "Betty had endured rumors of her supposed aloofness from social life, her uncooperativeness with reporters, and her dominating attitude at the studio."

After ten months Betty was permitted to return to work for her next film, *The Farmer Takes a Wife*. At Fox Grable begged Zanuck to purchase the screen rights to the Broadway hit

*Gentlemen Prefer Blondes,* convinced the Anita Loos musical would revive her career. Zanuck purchased the rights, but without informing Betty he announced that Marilyn Monroe would star. Monroe had just made international headlines by appearing nude in a calendar photograph. When reporters asked Betty how she felt about being dumped, she shrugged her shoulders: "Any number of girls do what I do. After all, Mr. Zanuck and Mr. Schenck are the bosses." But Betty was furious.

Preparing for *The Farmer Takes a Wife,* Grable learned Travilla refused to work with her and personally phoned him at home. She persuaded him to work again with her, and promised to behave herself this time. Betty realized she was living on borrowed time. Every day after work she withdrew to her dressing room, where Billie waited to confer on their strategy for avoiding a showdown with the Fox legal staff. Billie would arrive at 2:00 P.M. and remain until the end of the day's shooting.

"Is my mother coming today?" Betty would ask her costumer, Josephine Brown. If not, she'd reach for her hidden bottle of liquor and, in the isolation of her dressing room, listen to music on the radio, a cigarette going constantly. She would make her regular two phone calls a day home to help supervise. Then she'd turn to her favorite pastime—handicapping ponies. She kept in constant touch with the bookies.

Grable's studio contacts were now confined to a small group of loyal wardrobe women who had worked with her over the years. During a pause in filming, she'd drive them to her home for a quick lunch of sandwiches and coffee.

No longer counted among Zanuck's inner circle of stars, Betty Grable was subjected to constant harassment as studio personnel monitored and documented her every unexcused tardiness or absence. Her squabbles with the costume designers were causing expensive delays in filming, and the legal department deluged her with letters declaring her in violation of contract. Despite these pressures, the studio still expected Betty to prepare for her role with hours of dance rehearsals, prerecording sessions, script memorization, costume fittings, publicity photo sessions, and press interviews.

Both Betty and Marilyn Monroe named what they feared most during periods of "fallen grace"—the publicity department. Without Zanuck's protection, publicists had the power to destroy Grable in the press by planting ugly rumors to sway public opinion. A cruel and powerful weapon, it would batter and weaken her emotionally. The embattled star who had earned over $100 million for Fox now fled between scenes to the sanctuary of her dressing room, where she locked the door and cried. By the time she was called for the next scene, Betty, reinforced by a couple of vodka and tonics, emerged composed and determined not to give the studio an excuse to suspend her.

Robert Wagner recalls, "We used to walk around the lots and streets and watch Grable film. During *My Blue Heaven* she was standing there with the stomach sort of sticking out. She was just sort of relaxed and then they put that slate in front of her and the stomach came in and the shoulders went back—and boom! The magic came on."

"Who the hell's that punk staring at me?" Betty said to the unit manager, pointing at Wagner. But soon the two became fast friends. She often invited him into her dressing room, where he would sit at her feet and stare. "I was in total awe of her," he admitted.

Betty agreed to star in Preston Sturges's *The Beautiful Blonde From Bashful Bend* against her better instincts. She worried her fans would not accept her as a tough, gun-toting saloon singer of the Old West. But she was aware of Sturges's brilliance and hoped he was the one man who could help her graduate from showgirl to actress-comedienne. She also suspected the studio planned to suspend her if she refused the part. When the press got wind of her reservations about the role, she said, "I'm a frustrated perfectionist. I worry about everything." Then she contradicted herself, "No, I never study a script. I just worry about my hair and clothes."

No sooner had production begun than Betty's suspicions were confirmed. Sturges planned to satirize her as "queen of the turn-of-the-century showgirls," just as Lubitsch and Preminger had done with her in *That Lady in Ermine*. When she complained to studio brass she was told to stop being temperamental. After all, hadn't Sturges's *The Miracle of Morgan's Creek* helped Betty Hutton's career? *Beautiful Blonde* was Sturges's first Technicolor effort and last American film. He left for Europe, where he wrote and directed another disaster, *Les Carnets du Major Thompson,* released in America as *The French They Are a Funny Race.* Sturges admitted that *Beautiful Blonde* was inspired by the Mae West–W. C. Fields classic *My Little Chickadee.*

Unlike the slick and witty *Chickadee,* however, *Beautiful Blonde* was heavily slapstick. Fox was embarrassed and Grable mortified—this would be the worst turkey of her career. Grable's innate vulgarity had been camouflaged in previous films by her dame-with-a-heart-of-gold impersonations. Preston Sturges turned her into a tough, amoral, pistol-packing broad. "Freddie" shoots a judge in the rear, lands in jail, talks like a hick, and masquerades as a schoolteacher named Helen Swandumper, who tells two students, "You'll learn geography if it croaks ya!" Ordering the terrified boys to put inkwells on their heads, Grable shouts, "Freeze!" and shoots, exploding both bottles and sending the ink streaming down over their petrified faces.

Audiences had never seen this darker side of Grable. They were confused by the gauche, unfunny satire. Zanuck said Sturges "crucified her in it. We previewed it in Pomona and during the showing I left the theater and walked around the block ten times. God, I didn't know what to do."

In her hand-wringing interview with Louella Parsons, Betty unintentionally came off as a classic victim. "I didn't want to do it," she said in anguish, "but I never interfered with my studio. I never read a script until it's ready and I always leave the selection of story, directions *[sic]* and cost to Darryl Zanuck—for whom I have great respect. But if he ever gives me Preston Sturges again, you'll hear Grable's voice!"

Bosley Crowther wrote in *The New York Times:* "One might say that Betty Grable, as the beautiful blonde, is no great help since she shows a peculiar reluctance for the rowdy-dow of knock-down drag-out farce. For one reason or another Mr.

Sturges has not got out of her what he got out of Betty Hutton in *The Miracle of Morgan's Creek.*"

Betty had few friends to comfort her as her rank in the cruelly exact echelon of box-office stars was steadily eroded by flops and the audience's preference for "message" movies.

"I don't remember my mother ever socializing with anyone she ever worked with," Jessie said. But Jessie would be along the day Betty went to visit Joan Crawford.

# CHAPTER 13

Shortly after arriving at Joan Crawford's, Jessie wandered into the bedroom of Joan's adopted son, Christopher. There she saw a strange-looking harness attached to his bed. Naturally curious, Jessie studied it carefully before turning to her mother for an explanation. But Betty, who said she was "well aware" of its existence, merely shrugged her shoulders and said, "It's not much. Drop it." But it was "much." It was the same harness that figured so prominently in Christina Crawford's gothic-styled biography, *Mommie Dearest*.

Joan Crawford once admitted, "There were times when I was too strict. I expected them to appreciate their advantages. I was a strict disciplinarian—perhaps too strict. But my God, without discipline what is life? I hate to generalize but I don't think stars of my time should have had children."

Grable, like Crawford, shared a peculiar and distorted view of sex. They seemed to find sex unwholesome and repugnant despite the fact that both women spent their lifetimes in secret and not-so-secret premarital and extramarital affairs. Both Joan and Betty had been psychologically abused by their parents and in turn victimized their young children.

"Sex plays a tremendously important part in every person's life," Crawford blasted, when Betty's friend and costar (in *How to Marry a Millionaire)* Marilyn Monroe appeared at an awards dinner scantily clad. "People are interested in it, intrigued with it. But they don't like to see it flaunted in their faces. Monroe should be told that the public likes provocative feminine personalities but it also likes to know, underneath it all, the actresses are ladies."

And Marilyn, not to be outdone in public, rose to the occasion with her rebuttal: "I think the thing that hit me hardest is that it came from her [Crawford]. I've always admired her for being a wonderful mother—for taking four children and giving them a fine home. Who, better than I, knows what it means to homeless little ones?"

Since Betty and Harry provided absolutely no consistent home life for Vickie and Jessie, the girls sought love elsewhere. "At the school we went to in Beverly Hills, Mia Farrow was in my sister's class and I used to go over to their home all the time," Jessie remembers. "And Ricardo Montalban's son—I used to go over to their house too. Then there was Jeanne Crain, who was always pregnant. But my parents didn't associate with my friends' parents. My mother wasn't interested in what those people had to offer. But then my parents were never together either."

Jessica returned from school one day to find the servants whispering her mother was ill. When asked what was wrong, Betty explained to her daughter that she had miscarried. Jessica learned years later her mother did not have a miscarriage. She suffered from the aftermath of another abortion, perhaps the result of a one-night stand with one of the many male companions she brought home with her.

Betty always kept photographs of Jackie Coogan in her bedroom closet, Jessie said, adding ruefully that Betty never bothered to display any photos of Jessie as a child. When Jessie inquired about this, reasonably pointing out that Maureen

O'Sullivan, Mia Farrow's mother, had baby pictures all over the place, Betty said, "I didn't have any pictures taken of you as a child."

Betty Grable was glad to be working on a major musical with Marilyn Monroe—*How to Marry a Millionaire.* Betty had been feuding with Fox, which in 1952 tried to force her to appear in *Blaze of Glory*, the first dramatic part offered her in eleven years. She was to play a prostitute involved in a Communist plot. Betty regarded this as another act of sabotage by Fox, designed to annhiliate her at the box office. "I wouldn't work in a picture like that," she said. "I want to work in movies I can take my daughters to."

"Are you going to do it?" Travilla asked her during a stormy period at the studio that was ignited by her defiance of Zanuck.

"I am not! I can't do it—it's too much *acting.*"

"But you *are* an actress," Travilla pointed out. "Oh, honey, you *need* this show." Betty stonewalled Fox, taking a salary suspension lasting eight months. Retitled *Pickup on South Street*, the film finally went to Jean Peters after it had been turned down by Shelley Winters. Betty defied Fox again when Fox tried to loan her out to Columbia for *The Pleasure Is All Mine.* A Hollywood columnist sniped, "Grable's the laziest gal to achieve stardom. The many suspensions she took from 20th over a period of twelve years were never due to temperament. She just didn't want to work because (1) she wanted to go to the Del Mar races with Harry James, (2) she wanted to go to the Bay Meadows races and cheer on their thoroughbred Big Noise, who won a $100,000 purse last year, and (3) she just wanted to stay home with her two girls and Harry James." It had the ring of studio flak. The Fox publicity department was chipping away at her again.

Then, suddenly, Betty Grable could do no wrong. Fox needed her for *How to Marry a Millionaire.* The dowager love goddess—Grable—and the pretender to the throne—Monroe—in the same film: a casting inspiration. And it was good for Grable too, as she was the first to acknowledge. She gave one of her best performances.

When it was announced Betty's costars for *How to Marry a Millionaire* would be Marilyn Monroe and Lauren Bacall, the talk from the Polo Lounge to the El Padrino was that the battle of the blondes was about to begin.

Marilyn arrived late for the first day of shooting, but Lauren and Betty were already made up and dressed for their first scene with her. The two veteran stars waited patiently. Two hours passed. Bacall, under great pressure from the daily ordeal of watching her husband, Humphrey Bogart, waste away from cancer, finally complained, "What the hell is she doing? I'm ready—why can't she be?"

Grable said quietly, "It's her time. She's coming up. She's coming right up there as the biggest star—and it's *her* time. So let's not worry about it. Let's listen to music. Want some coffee? No sweat. I'm gonna slip this dress off so it doesn't wrinkle. I've got plenty of time. After all, they're paying me."

Another time during filming Betty received a call informing her that Jessie had been injured in a fall from her horse. Betty quickly left the set and rushed home. That evening, Betty received a phone call from a woman who spoke in a strangely halting, breathy whisper that was barely audible.

"Betty, how's Jessica?"

"She's fine. But who is this?"

After a long pause the voice answered, "It's Marilyn."

"Marilyn who?" demanded Grable.

"Marilyn Monroe," she whispered. Betty suddenly realized Marilyn wanted friendship. There would be, in the coming days, many gestures of kindness from Marilyn, and Betty was extremely touched. Betty and Marilyn enjoyed a warm and satisfying relationship. Though both women preferred the company of men, they respected each other and were comfortable exchanging confidences. Marilyn had been a star-struck fan of the forties movie queen. Now she lost no opportunity to study Betty first-hand.

The filming of *How to Marry a Millionaire* proceeded smoothly. At first, Bacall, Grable, and Monroe maintained a polite distance from each other. Bacall remained cool, formally courteous, and aloof. One day, however, she let her hair down with Charles LeMaire, who was supervising the fitting of her costume. Bacall asked, "Where the hell is that horn player's wife?"

Bacall wrote in 1978: "Betty Grable was a funny, outgoing woman, totally professional and easy. Marilyn was frightened, insecure—trusted only her coach and was always late. She had no meanness in her—no bitchery. She just had to concentrate on herself and the people who were there for her. Grable and I decided we'd try to make it easier for her—make her feel she could trust us. I think she finally did."

Travilla never heard Betty utter an unkind word about Marilyn. He said that Betty admired a Monroe gown he had created. "Boy," Betty said, "that girl's dynamite. She's beautiful. And she's gorgeous in that dress. Bill, why don't you do one like that for me?"

Thanks to Marilyn Monroe, Betty Grable would at last attend a big Hollywood premiere. She always shunned them, saying, "I am the furthest possible thing from what a star should be. I just once would like to feel up to going to a premiere and enjoying the bright lights. I would like to know how it is to yearn for a white mink coat and a diamond brooch—to put them on and then go, bow graciously, speak into the mike, and sign autographs. That is how a star should behave. If I tried it, my slip would show and I would run like a rabbit on seeing the crowd."

When Monroe complained to Betty that Joe DiMaggio refused to accompany her to the film's premiere, Grable agreed to go. "I'll not only take you but I'll also pick you up and drive you there myself."

Draped in a white mink stole she had "borrowed" from Wardrobe, Betty pulled up in her Cadillac at Marilyn's apartment and honked the horn. Marilyn leaned out of a window and hollered, "I'll be right down, honey!"

As Betty would later tell Jessie, at the post-premiere dinner party Marilyn complained she was unable to remove her elbow-length white satin gloves. Betty, acting as the dutiful big sister, pulled and tugged at Marilyn's gloves until her hands were freed and she could resume her dinner.

Soon after *How to Marry a Millionaire,* 20th Century–Fox abruptly announced to the press that its contract with "Miss Grable" had been terminated "by mutual agreement." No details of the settlement were disclosed nor were any reasons specified for the sudden cancellation. The official version had it that Betty wished to pursue a nightclub career and spend more time with Harry and the girls. The truth was that Zanuck was fed up with her histrionics and exasperated with her performance in *How to Marry a Millionaire.* He accused her of trying to upstage the other stars with her terrible hairstyles—which he felt were deliberately devised to draw more attention to herself and antagonize him. Her cut was in fact unstylish, especially compared with Bacall's trendy coif and the sleek hairdo that highlighted Marilyn's fantastic allure. Perhaps Grable hung on to her outmoded hairdo as the last vestige of the power that had been hers.

Zanuck had miscalculated in writing off Betty's performance in *Millionaire.* He lavished top billing on Marilyn Monroe, but it was Grable who was singled out when *The New York Times* verdict came in. Bosley Crowther, dean of U.S. movie critics for decades on end, wrote, "As a breezy mistress Grable is the funniest of the ladies. Her offscreen capitulation to forest ranger Rory Calhoun is by far the most sensible and painless bit of feminine behavior in the film."

Betty Grable said goodbye to a few friends at Fox, collected some items from her dressing room, and braced herself to face the press outside her quarters. Her firing had become a media event.

She walked briskly toward the photographers and reporters. Trim, sexy, spirited as a filly, her short blond hair bobbing in a cute ponytail, Betty wore a white sleeveless summer dress that showed off her creamy tan. Clutching her pillbox purse, Grable flashed a brave smile. "If Harry wants me," she said, "I'll join his band. But he's the boss. We've been so happy for ten years, he might think it wouldn't be good for us to work together. Whatever he says goes. I got a kick out of playing a straight comedienne in *Millionaire* with no singing or dancing. But at heart I'm a musical-comedy hoofer—and everybody should stick to his own line. I'm no great shakes as an actress—I've never been within gunshot of an Oscar, but I think I've entertained a few people." She waved a final goodbye as she headed for her car.

Staff publicists at 20th Century–Fox, who had obediently scorned or praised her over the years, on Darryl Zanuck's whim, now sickeningly eulogized, "She shed a little tear, driving off the 20th lot for the last time. Then she promptly put all those good years behind her."

The few who saw her off that day detected no hint of tears in Betty Grable's clear blue eyes. What they did see was the determination of a star who was not down yet.

# CHAPTER
# 14

Actor Max Showalter, a friend to both Grable and Monroe, who worked with both of them at various times, remembered, "During the filming of *Niagara,* Marilyn sometimes invited me into her dressing room or her hotel room for a drink. After closing the door behind her she began to cross-examine me about any of 'Betty's secrets' that might help her to improve her sex image. I keep seeing so much of Betty in Marilyn," Max said.

"Now, how does she walk?" Marilyn asked, begging Max to demonstrate a poised, sexy saunter.

"It was all Betty," Max said. "Marilyn took everything she could get. Even Betty's way of talking. If you look today at some of the older pictures of Betty's—Marilyn had studied them and Marilyn then took it even further—the moves, the look, all Grable."

This curious disclosure by Showalter reveals Marilyn's practice of emulating and even miming stars of the past and present in her assault on stardom. It also reveals the motivating factor in Marilyn's desire to cultivate a friendship with Betty. Betty distrusted everybody, especially other female stars. But Marilyn somehow managed to captivate Grable and gain her trust—as she scrutinized and analyzed Betty's every move like some insatiable Eve Harrington vampire.

Monroe continued to quiz Max on Grable during the filming of *Bus Stop*. Monroe's immortal rendition of "That Old Black Magic" owes a clear debt to Betty Grable, not to mention the more obvious debt to Kim Stanley's Broadway showstopper.

One night, Marilyn and Joe DiMaggio came to dinner at Betty and Harry's. A great baseball fan, Harry was delirious. Their gorgeous blonde wives relegated to the benches, Harry James and Joe DiMaggio talked baseball all night long.

Betty and Marilyn welcomed the opportunity for a heart-to-heart. By now, Marilyn knew her marriage was failing. Monroe told Grable she was having trouble falling asleep at night. As she would also complain to her studio friend Bill Smith, Joe's nightly nocturnal mania for "watching the boob tube" until five in the morning made it difficult for her to bear the pressures at Fox.

One night Marilyn called Betty in a panic. As Betty later related to friends, Marilyn complained of physical abuse. On a number of occasions, Marilyn fled for sanctuary from her own embattled home to Betty's embattled home. Whatever the crisis, Marilyn Monroe was always welcome at Betty's. The blonde goddesses of the forties and fifties were sisters under the skin, bonded together by the public's glorification and a hopeless sadness within.

When he *was* around—and that was all the time less and less—Harry James seems never to have physically or verbally abused his children. Jessie says her father only once lifted his hand to her: "We were living on Doheny Road. And me and my sister were doing something naughty. So he came upstairs and he took us and made us pull our pants down. Then he went 'smack' to Vicki and then 'smack' to me. That was the last time he ever touched us. He never, never yelled at us."

Betty Ritz remembers the time she and her children accompanied the entire James family to Lake Tahoe, where Harry and Betty were headlining at Harrah's. Once settled in, James proceeded to escort—in public—flashy showgirls on his nightly rounds of casino gambling tables. When Betty shrieked in protest, Harry ominously warned her he expected her to remain behind in the hotel "or else."

Near the end of the engagement, an informant told Harry "the gals"—Betty Grable and Betty Ritz—had been spotted in the company of a handsome young casino bartender as they were boarding a pleasure boat for a midnight ride on the lake. James confronted Grable the following morning. In screams echoing down the hall, Betty denied everything. James tore into her. The beating left her face swollen with Harry's hand marks, which turned into purple-blue bruises.

Later, with Betty Ritz, Grable wept as she made plans to cancel the rest of her run at Harrah's. How could she go on, looking like this? Ritz managed to calm her down by demonstrating how Betty could go on after all. Ritz applied stage makeup heavily and assured Grable that various filters in the stagelights would camouflage the bruises and swellings. Grable went on with the show. But it was a nightmare not too uncommon for Hollywood's most popular couple. It seemed they lived a film scenario filled with lustful passion and spy intrigue, followed by scenes of jealous rages and recriminations.

Understandably nervous about facing her violent husband again, Grable knew she eventually had to. Betty Ritz, ever the fearless friend, agreed to accompany her. In the scene that followed, Harry accused Grable of "screwing around" on him, called her a "cheap slut," and showed every sign of slugging her again until Betty Ritz spoke up loudly corroborating Grable's contention that she was innocent of the alleged peccadillo. The truth of the matter, Betty Ritz later admitted to numerous friends, was that the two Bettys often flirted with bartenders and musicians. Taxi drivers, truck drivers, and bartenders always drew special attention from Grable.

Grable became involved with a backup drummer to cult nightclub singer Frances Faye. When his wife learned of it, she sank her fingernails into his light-brown-skinned body for his fellow musicians and Faye to see.

Jessie says "slippery-looking types" occasionally visited her mother at their home when she was still married to her absentee Harry. Cursory introductions were made before Betty hustled a new boyfriend up to her bedroom. In *Meet Me After the Show,* Grable was surrounded by a number of very handsome, scantily clad musclemen during the musical production number "No-Talent Joe." After the filming, Grable, who was very excited by all the hunks, invited them over to her house along with Betty Ritz, where they partied until the wee hours of the morning.

The Jameses bought a ranch and liked it so much they soon bought another nearby. Betty and Harry became the toast of the fan magazines, whose editors loved to show them luxuriating on their ranches. They talked even further of expansion in ranching, but Harry's gambling debts quickly made it difficult to maintain the large properties the couple already owned. It fell to Betty to lease out the white elephants ruining her sleep and depleting her resources. With their combined gambling debts, the Jameses couldn't even meet their monthly expenses. Eventually both ranches had to be sold off just to cover Harry's appalling losses.

Billie, Betty Grable's independent mother, was still very much a part of the scene. She accompanied Harry and Betty on their annual trek to Del Mar. Billie thoroughly enjoyed the races, but it cannot be said that Harry enjoyed Billie. According to Jessie, he barely tolerated the old woman and tried never to socialize with her. Jessie says, "He *never* referred to Grandmother Billie." Jessie remembers she did not learn until her eighteenth year that her grandparents had divorced in 1939.

Bud worked as the Jameses' ranch manager for thoroughbred horses. Marjorie, as devoted to her father as Betty was, said it was Harry—not Betty—who made the suggestion to hire Bud to manage the ranches. "Conn Grable did not drink in the daytime," Marjorie said. "He did not drink after dinner. But her sure got his licks in *before* dinner. At one time Daddy may have had a problem, but I know that he had completely stopped."

Betty taught Jessie to address Billie as "Girl Donny" and Bud as "Boy Donny," because Vicki, at the age of five, had been unable to pronounce *grandmother* and *grandfather* correctly. Jessie had no difficulty pronouncing them herself, but was nevertheless forced to use the nicknames convenient for Vicki.

Betty Grable took good care of her mother. She bought Billie a house in Beverly Hills, not far from the Beverly Wilshire Hotel, on Rodeo Drive. Billie could hold her head high when she ran into old friends.

Though Betty ranted in front of her daughter about how she'd been tortured as a girl by Billie—the jailing in the bathroom was a favorite horror story—Jessie liked to visit her grandmother at 275 Rodeo Drive. At Girl Donny's house Jessie loved to explore the musty-odored, antique-filled rooms with dark mahogany-paneled walls and strange portraits of people with big eyes that seemed to follow her as she moved.

Upstairs in Billie's bedroom, bright with chintz and billowing gauze curtains, stood a bar built to her specifications. Her handicap now made it difficult for her to go up and down the stairs as often as she needed refills.

Billie complained of leg and hip pains, which Jessie claims were the result of a slowly degenerating arthritic condition. Billie became dependent on the support of a leg brace and, eventually, a cane. She rarely strayed from home, where she was happy in the company of her white toy poodle, Lover Boy. Ever since Betty bought the pet for her, Billie regularly engaged in full conversations with Lover Boy. The dog formed the pampered center of Billie's lonely life. She never permitted strangers around him. "I don't know whose Lover Boy he was," her daughter Marjorie quipped.

Billie had an old car parked in her garage. When she got behind the wheel, which was seldom, she never drove faster than twenty miles an hour. Betty was livid—she hated it when people were feeble and slow. "My mother used to wonder why my grandmother would never take that car out and really use it," Jessie recalls. "Mother would really tell her off." As Billie's dependence on Betty inexorably increased with age, Betty became intolerant and testy, often totally ignoring Billie or chewing her out brutally.

"We were driving and my mother had been drinking," Jessie said. "We went over one of those speed bumps and my grandmother slammed forward and bruised her arm. Wow, was she mad. But my mother couldn't have cared less."

Betty loathed her mother's maddening dinnertime habit of slowly chewing each bite of food a hundred times. Long after the others had left the table and the dirty dishes had been cleared, Billie sat there doggedly masticating.

Conn Grable was the kind of grandfather who always had a warm smile for his grandchildren. He affectionately addressed Betty as "Babe" and Marjorie as "Futz."

Betty took her father to a hospital in the valley the night he collapsed. By the time they reached the hospital, Bud had lapsed into semiconsciousness. Betty demanded immediate emergency attention for the old man, who was obviously dying, but the medical staff insisted she complete the necessary admission forms. Conn Grable died on January 25, 1954, at 1:40 A.M., hunched in a wheelchair in admissions. Cause of death was listed as "renal insufficiency complicated by additional factors of arteriola nephro-sclerosis and gouty nephritis"—in other words, alcoholism.

During the brief period of mourning, Marjorie stopped by Billie's home one evening. In the bedroom, she glanced at Billie's open engagement book. The pages had not been turned since the day Conn died. On that page Billie had written, "Today Bud died—the only man I ever loved."

Betty would never forgive the hospital. She held its neglect directly responsible for her father's death. Though she loved him deeply, her bitterness over the cruelty of his dying and her hatred of doctors would forever cloud her memories of her father.

Just when it seemed Harry's mounting debts would ruin them, Columbia Pictures offered Betty a starring role in *Three for the Show.* It sounded heady—Jack Lemmon, Marge and Gower Champion, Hoagy Carmichael tunes, and George Gershwin ballads. A glamorous comeback seemed in the offing. But Grable was wasted. Though she'd dieted her figure back into top dancing form, it was Gower Champion who got all the big dance numbers. The few standard songs given to Betty were incompatible with her trademark style.

Meanwhile, Fox was mired in legal entanglements with Marilyn Monroe, who had refused to report to work for her next assignment, *How to Be Very, Very Popular*, on the grounds it offered little promise of establishing her as a "serious actress." Marilyn was weighing various offers, including one from Aristotle Onassis who, as a major investor in the Monaco gambling casino, decided that what was best for the tiny principality in drawing worldwide attention was to have the Prince marry a real-life movie star. *Look* magazine's Gardner Cowles, Jr., acting on behalf of Onassis, asked Marilyn if she would be interested in marrying Prince Rainier of Monaco. As Monroe mulled over the proposal Cowles asked, "Do you think the prince will marry you?" Marilyn replied, "Give me two days alone with him and of course he'll want to marry me." Marilyn was eventually scratched from the list of potential candidates in favor of Grace Kelly.

When it was clear to Fox that Marilyn had no intention of returning, the studio offered her part to Betty. She agreed to costar with Sheree North, a blonde groomed to replace Monroe just as Monroe had been brought in to unseat Grable. Despite her versatility, fine musical talents, and great show of promise, North unfortunately entered the studio system at its moment of collapse from the impact of television. It was Sheree, not Betty, whom Fox featured in the big production number "Shake, Rattle and Roll." Betty looked splendid in her brief costumes, but her part was strictly second fiddle to Sheree. The film was a disaster.

Distraught, Betty phoned her sister and tearfully admitted her film career was over. To the press she announced, "From now on, I will concentrate on my theater and nightclub engagements." Bosley Crowther wrote in *The New York Times:* "Demonstrations of *How to Be Very, Very Popular* strongly indicate that movie titles sometimes can be very excessive. For this farce about the trivial trials of two burlesque chorines . . . is long on confusion, flip dialogue and lovely limbs and short on inventive comedy and story content. Sheree North, as the somnambulistic blonde, and Betty Grable as her equally blonde, wise-cracking partner, are a treat to the male eye."

Singer Johnnie Ray said, "The studio was trying to put Marilyn into some kind of submission by grooming Sheree North as the new 'blonde' on the lot." But more significant, it had never been clearer that the Betty Grable musical was a relic of the past. Zanuck, prompted by the reality of a ninety-percent tax bracket, quit Fox to enter independent production. Replacing him was Buddy Adler, a man whose undistinguished contributions signaled the end of the quality filmmaking that distinguished 20th Century–Fox in the 1940s.

The Grable musicals had enjoyed a popularity unequaled in film history. Other studios tried to emulate the formula but none could ever duplicate the long succession of box-office hits Betty Grable single-handedly engineered during her twelve-year reign at Fox. Her enormous box-office clout allowed the studio's financing of ambitious pictures like *The Razor's Edge.* Zanuck once promised that if his much-heralded *Wilson,* which cost a then unprecedented $5 million, failed at the box office, he would "never again make a picture without Betty Grable." Now, as Grable retired, Zanuck reflected on her unique longevity in musicals: "During World War II she became the GI pin-up girl. But the amazing thing is that she kept on going! Fourteen years at the top of the exhibitors' poll! No one else reigned, I would say, even half the time. Fourteen years and then she dropped off totally. She had a great run for her money."

Samuel Goldwyn called and offered her the role of Adelaide in *Guys and Dolls,* but Betty upped her asking price and refused to consider several of Goldwyn's compromise offers. Incensed, Goldwyn terminated negotiations and announced Vivian Blaine would recreate her Broadway role on the screen.

Betty found work in television in a Mario Lanza spectacular, but as far as the critics were concerned, her highly touted debut fizzled. Unlike her chum Lucille Ball, Betty Grable was one refugee from Hollywood who did not find a second career in television, try as she might. High-paying offers to appear in

Las Vegas nightclubs as a solo act or with Harry James were more impressive.

"I've made more friends in Vegas than I ever did here in California," Grable offered in her last filmland interview. "And besides, Harry and I get to spend more time together. It really is the best place in the world."

After a long and successful Vegas stint with Harry, Betty took her nostalgic solo revue, *Memories,* from Hollywood's Sunset Strip and Moulin Rouge and finally to Puerto Rico. The act became such a hit Betty decided to move to Vegas, enrolling her daughters in a Catholic school there, where they faced a difficult period of readjustment.

Richard Allan, a young Fox contract player, volunteered to help Betty move to Vegas from her home on North Beverly Drive. Hitching up a trailer filled with personal belongings and selected pieces of furniture—Betty placed most of the antiques and silver in storage—Grable drove out of Beverly Hills, leaving behind her film career, her mother, and Marjorie. She was as optimistic as Billie had been the day she left St. Louis for Hollywood in 1929.

# CHAPTER 15

On the highway to Las Vegas Richard Allan was struck by Betty's crude attempt at frugality. Wouldn't it have been easier and safer to ship all those things? Absolutely not, Betty insisted, citing "prohibitive costs." The costs couldn't have amounted to a fraction of what she regularly spent on friends like Allan, the lucky recipient of tasteful and expensive gifts from Betty.

Her new $100,000 home was situated behind the Tropicana Hotel. Betty had always despised Beverly Hills snobbery. Now she abandoned all pretense of elegance. The house on North Beverly had looked like the home of a star, but in Vegas Betty headed straight for Woolworth's and bought plastic dishes, plastic glasses, plastic tablecloths, and aluminum flatware. Not one photograph or movie memento was displayed in her sterile desert retreat. Systematically wiping out her past, Grable had no intention of entertaining elaborately or maintaining a movie-star mystique. "Come hell or high water," she said, "I'm going to do the things and behave in the manner *I* want."

She failed to recognize how quickly one could go to hell in a place like Vegas. She never needed the powers of self-discipline, cultivated over a lifetime in show business, more—nor realized the fact less.

Las Vegas, gambling capital of the world, endures unbearable summer heat and freezing cold winters. But the desert community gratified Betty's insatiable gambling thirst, which by now bore all the marks of irreversible addiction. Here the self-exiled movie queen remained free to haunt the bars and casinos without fear of scandal or public criticism. The citizens of Las Vegas are not only good nightclub audiences, but loyal and devoted fans of the fading stars who often choose to live among them. In all its splendid and profound barrenness, the desert promised, at least temporarily, to offer the peaceful era of tranquility Betty desperately sought. But as she baked to an unhealthy crisp in the blazing sun she loved so well, the desert seemed to mirror and reinforce her emotional and physical emptiness.

Betty began her daily golf game at six in the morning, before the sun made it impossible for her to play. She lunched with local women friends and played poker or bridge in the afternoon. Two evenings a week were devoted to bowling and two to catching the latest lounge or nightclub acts. After the shows she would rush to the casino tables and roulette wheels and remain there until dawn.

Studio power games had absorbed Grable's energies for years. Now her skills for challenge and competition found release at the gaming tables. "We had to play games with her," Betty Ritz said. "She loved games. When she was playing she got excited. She had to play it and win it. If you doddered around in poker Betty would scold, 'Oh my God. Don't you know what three kings are? And what three aces are? Or a full house?'" During one bowling tournament, she emerged the champion. Accepting her trophy, Betty said, "This beats winning an Oscar any day."

Marjorie said, "She had very close contacts with women there. She had some *awfully* nice and supportive friends." These included Toni Clark, widow of Wilbur Clark and former owner of the Desert Inn gambling casino, and singer Keeley Smith, then one of Vegas's favorite acts. Betty and Keeley often shared a quiet afternoon, lolling about the pool, drinking, and sunbathing.

Harry James was rarely in evidence. Though he and Betty were still married and living together, Harry came home only long enough to rest and change clothes before hurrying off to late-afternoon rehearsals. He worked from 9:00 P.M. until 5:00 A.M. He still gambled heavily and embarrassed Betty regularly with his public philandering. With the girls away at school, Betty, having learned to tolerate Harry's excessive indulgences, soon found time to indulge herself in a number of romantic and not-so-romantic encounters. Sometimes, after an all-night gambling session, Grable would let her hair down in a darkened predawn bar as she spoke crudely of her predilection for macho truck driver and bartender types, admitting also that though she found sexual penetration especially painful, she did enjoy engaging in fellatio.

Richard Allan became a frequent escort. Stunningly handsome, he appeared in minor roles in *Niagara, With a Song in My Heart,* and *The Snows of Kilimanjaro.* Fox finally subjected him to routine work as a studio model testing various new CinemaScope makeups before terminating his contract. After two years in Europe, appearing in several German films, Allan worked in a Las Vegas revue headlined by Grable.

"She was so good with her mother," Allan said, "yet with her daughters she was nasty, hard, and cold. And boy, she could really clamp down on them—and other people too. The least little thing could greatly upset her and then she'd really cut loose.

"I think she was unnecessarily strict with her children. Very strict and very tough-speaking. If there was a ballgame, a dance, or any popular school event—and if they had even mildly misbehaved—they were simply not allowed to go. And that was a frequent occurrence.

"She wanted them to appreciate everything she had done for them. It was always all right for her to criticize and poke fun at herself—but the girls couldn't say a word." Allan was dining with Betty and the girls at an Italian restaurant when the girls impishly poked fun at Betty's chubby hands. Nostrils flaring, Betty squelched the good-humored teasing and lashed out, "For your information little girls, these *chubby* hands have made a lot of money." She shook her clenched fists at them threateningly.

Jeff Parker, a young dancer from Iowa, was another escort and sometime coworker. "I was very much in love with Betty Grable," he said, "not only as a young fan from Iowa, very star-struck, but emotionally involved with the woman. She was at heart a chorus girl who'd made it—caring and charismatic." Betty told Parker, "If you want to make it with me honey, fine. I think you're attractive. Come on, let's go to bed. If not, that's fine baby—now let's go on. Life is going on—we're walking in time here."

Why did she stay married to her absentee husband, Jeff asked her. "Honey, he's my man and he's got enough for me, for you, and for every faggot in this show."

Garish Las Vegas served as a virtual hotbed for the disintegrating James family. The girls, cut off from Billie and Marjorie, who had provided some semblance of a family life, were now sentenced to a restricted Catholic school environment and their mother's continuing outbursts.

Jessie began to rebel and fight back, deliberately provoking her mother to angry extremes. "She was really, in her own way, like a rebel herself," Jessie comments. "She was real tough on herself. My mother saw me going out and doing the same things she used to do and she hated me because I reminded her of herself. But I'm sure she loved me—I think there was a lot of love there."

A very defiant Jessica prompted school officials to report to Betty: "Today, Mrs. James, Jessica failed to attend her classes and when she was present she disrupted the class." And: "Today, Mrs. James, Jessica failed to attend her classes. Later she was found in another part of the school grounds, smoking! It's absolutely imperative that you speak to your daughter and put a stop to these disruptions; otherwise, we shall be forced to terminate her enrollment here."

One of Vicki's teachers reported to Betty: "Victoria was caught passing a lurid note to a fellow classmate, written in her own hand!"

"Can you imagine her writing dirty notes in class?" Betty screamed to her visiting friend Betty Ritz. "Just wait until she gets home! I'll fix her—the little tramp!"

"In many ways," Ritz said later, "Vickie was much more a problem to Betty than Jessie." Betty, certain Vicki was "fooling around," kept a midnight vigil as she waited for the young woman to return home from a date. In the darkened living room, peering through the window blinds, Betty finally saw her suspicions confirmed: Vicki kissed her boyfriend good night at the front door. Before Vicki had a chance to remove the key from the lock, Betty lunged from the shadows and seized her daughter, pushing Vicki up against the wall. She then proceeded to pull Vicki's hair, strike her, and rip her clothes. Vicki broke away and dashed for her room with Betty right behind her, landing a blow whenever she could.

Jessie, awakened by the screams, now found herself included in Betty's shouted threats—if they continued to defy house rules, they'd be thrown out into the streets, where they belonged. For days Betty harangued the girls. Both were given to understand they were expected to be on their own and out of her house by their eighteenth birthdays (and they were). Betty said she no longer wanted two such ingrates living under the same roof with her. "Start planning your move," she warned.

Betty vented her fury on Harry as well, but he learned to stay away and gamble, creating mounds of debts only she could pay. Now unemployed, Grable saw her savings and investments quickly dwindle away. On Christmas Day 1962 Grable returned to work, appearing with ex-lover Dan Dailey in a truncated version of *Guys and Dolls* at the Dunes Hotel. She was politely reviewed by Vegas critics.

Jessie did not go to college and she never knew if her parents cared. "It's like when my sister got married," she comments. "I knew then at her wedding that I'd never have a wedding. She was the one with all the advantages."

On April 4, 1964, Betty and Harry threw a party to announce

Victoria's impending marriage to a fellow University of Arizona student, William Wiley Bivens. The wedding was held in August.

Weeks before her eighteenth birthday, Jessie dropped a time bomb on her mother. She was pregnant without benefit of marriage. Too frightened to confide in Betty, Jessie asked her boyfriend, Ronald Yahner, to break the news. "Mrs. James," the seventeen-year-old courageously began, "I'm here to tell you that Jessie is pregnant and I'm the father."

Betty's calm reactions shocked Jessie. Betty offered emotional support and even expressed concern. She complimented Yahner for his decency in facing her, and she even thanked him. In due course, Ron kissed Jessie and returned home to his parents.

No sooner had the boy departed than Betty fell to pieces, yelling, "How could you ever have dared to sneak around behind my back to do such a thing? You better do whatever I say now while you're still under my roof. I'm only letting you stay here because of the condition you're in—and God—*look* at the condition you're in."

A few weeks later, Jessie, at home alone, began to hemorrhage. Unable to reach her mother, she rushed to the hospital, where she suffered a miscarriage. When Betty returned from the casinos that night, she appeared sympathetic, but within days again harped on Jessie's imminent ejection from home the instant she reached eighteen.

One night Betty became physically violent, hitting Jessie on the head and shoulders. Jessie ran for her bedroom, but Betty, in pursuit, pushed her to the floor and attempted to kick her. Jessie struggled up and pushed Betty against the wall. For a moment the two stood there glaring at each other, panting. "I bucked her authority for the first time," Jessie said. "I knew at that moment something important had happened between us—but I wasn't sure what." She would find out soon enough. Betty rushed to the phone and screamed at Harry: *"Take this girl out of my house. I want her out of here tonight!"* Like Jessie, Harry too had been thrown out of the house many times by Betty after a routine brawl, but he was luckier in that he could always escape to the bachelor pad he shared with Phil Harris. Without any fanfare or fuss and without even a fatherly lecture Harry James calmly collected his daughter and took her to the bachelor pad. Later he rented an apartment for Jessie in the same building and paid three months' rent in advance. After that, she was on her own.

For Jessie the full impact of that night of denial and rejection came on her eighteenth birthday, in May 1965, when neither parent acknowledged it. And neither Betty nor Harry attended her graduation from high school.

Jessie worked in a series of odd jobs, including waitressing at the Las Vegas International Hotel. She would become pregnant again, and move—alone—to Palm Springs for seven months before returning to Ronald Yahner. She would bear two children, Scott and Kelly Elizabeth. "And when I came back he married me. No, when I came back I stayed at my house. My mother laid a lot of things on me about being pregnant. Like, you better do what I say. I'm letting you stay here only because of the condition you're in."

Shortly before Jessie's eviction from her mother's house, Betty informed Jessie she was about to divorce Harry. "It didn't bother me," Jessie said. "He was never there anyhow. The only thing I felt was why didn't she get one a long time ago? I think it's stupid when two people stay together for the kids . . . It just makes everyone miserable."

Betty divorced Harry on October 8, 1965, after twenty-two years of marriage. The grounds for divorce: extreme cruelty. At private proceedings Betty was handed her decree in a sealed judgment by the Nevada State, Clark County district judge, John McKay. Her divorce attorney, Carl J. Christensen, called the settlement amicable and stated both parties would remain friendly. Betty did not ask for alimony.

Harry, then forty-nine, had earlier declared his band made $600,000 a year. Close friends, however, observed that Harry was in hock to the casino owners and would have to work for "more than a lifetime" to repay them. Muzzy Marcellino of Betty's band-singing days believed the James divorce may have been prompted by those gambling debts. Under law a divorced person is not legally responsible for the ex-spouse's debts.

"She cracked up over her marriage to Harry," Marjorie said.

"She was very upset about the divorce when she phoned me from Las Vegas. We talked for more than forty-five minutes and she was crying and saying, 'I can't get my damn wedding ring off!'"

Betty decided to give Dorothy Kilgallen, columnist for the *New York Journal-American*, a scoop on the divorce. Kilgallen observed Betty had not followed the Nevada divorce tradition of throwing the wedding ring away upon leaving the courthouse with divorce decree in hand. Betty did not tell Kilgallen the ring remained hopelessly stuck on her finger.

"It was completely amicable," Betty said, adding that the Jameses had chosen the day for the divorce to coincide with a newspaper strike to avoid publicity. "Harry and I agreed that neither of us would talk to reporters," she said, while talking to the nation's foremost reporter. "We'd been living in Las Vegas for seven years, and most of the time I was just a housewife. I even watched afternoon TV. It really wasn't a sudden thing. I thought it over for a long time and I talked it over with Harry. Our children are grown now with lives of their own. There was no reason to stay together for their sake.

"I'm not worried. God has been very good to me through the years, and I think he will be in the future . . . I'll never get married again—and I doubt if Harry will . . ."

But James did, at fifty-one. On January 8, 1968, he took a twenty-seven-year-old former Las Vegas showgirl and divorcee named Joan Boyd as his third wife. Duke Ellington's band, along with Harry's, turned the wedding reception into a swinging jam session. Betty Grable did not receive an invitation.

On July 18, 1969, the new Mrs. Harry James gave birth to Michael, a healthy six-pound fourteen-ounce baby. Harry boasted to musician friends that he once again had a male heir, reminding them also of his two grown sons from his first marriage to Louise Tobin.

Grable wrote Betty Ritz on August 21, 1968, from Honolulu, where she was appearing at a dinner theater (she capitalized all her *H*s, as in "Harry"):

> After Hearing I got the divorce I bought a real cute House on the

Adoring Betty, possessive yet indifferent Harry.
*Photo The Museum of Modern Art Film Stills Archives.*

• • • • • •

In *The Shocking Miss Pilgrim,* Betty foreshadowed the women's liberation movement of the sixties and seventies. Betty was unhappy with her costumes in this picture—they didn't show enough leg.
*Photo The Museum of Modern Art Film Stills Archives 20th Century–Fox.*

• • •

Betty fought for more revealing costumes in *Mother Wore Tights,* although they were inconsistent with the styles of the historical setting of the movie. A smash success, the movie pushed costar Dan Dailey to star status.
*Courtesy The Bettmann Archive.*

Four-year-old Vicki practices for Mom and Dad. Betty, however, jealous of Harry's obsession with music, privately discouraged her daughter's talent.
*Courtesy The Bettmann Archive.*

• • •

A family portrait: Vicki, Harry, baby Jessie, and Betty.
*Courtesy The Bettmann Archive.*

Betty clowning around with Bob Hope and Bing Crosby. Bing was a major stockholder of the Del Mar racetrack often frequented by Betty and Harry James. When their horse won a $100,000 purse, Betty declared that winning an Oscar could never equal the joy of winning a race.
*Photo The Museum of Modern Art Film Stills Archives.*

• • •

Exlover Tyrone Power visits Grable in her dressing room with Harry James during the production of *When My Baby Smiles at Me.*
*Photo The Museum of Modern Art Film Stills Archives.*

• • •

Betty and the girls gathered around the piano. They all desperately craved Harry James's approval and love.
*Courtesy The Bettmann Archive.*

Betty tried valiantly to enter Harry's musical world.
*Courtesy The Bettmann Archive.*

• • •

Betty passes her dancing talent along to her daughters at home at their ranch. Betty was soon to star in *The Beautiful Blonde from Bashful Bend.*
*Courtesy The Bettmann Archive.*

• • •

Betty and Harry at the ranch in 1949. He would always be her greatest love.
*Photo The Museum of Modern Art Film Stills Archives.*

The famous pin-up gives lessons to Jessie and Vicki.
*Photo The Museum of Modern Art Film Stills Archives.*

• • • • •

Grable and Monroe in *How to Marry a Millionaire.* Betty recognized herself as Marilyn's role model, which both pleased and angered her.
*Photo The Museum of Modern Art Film Stills Archives 20th Century–Fox.*

"Horses are our mutual interest, so the races are our opportunity," Betty told Hedda Hopper.
*Photo The Museum of Modern Art Film Stills Archives.*

• • •

Guests at Walter Winchell's birthday party. (*Left to right*) Standing: Betty Grable, Marilyn Monroe, Walter Winchell, Jane Russell; seated: Lucille Ball, songwriter Jimmy McHugh, Louella O. Parsons, Al Ritz.
*Courtesy Reggie Drew Denton.*

Betty struts her stuff in her last film for Fox. *How to Be Very, Very Popular,* with costar Sheree North. Marilyn Monroe had turned Betty's part down.
*Photo The Museum of Modern Art Film Stills Archives.*

• • •

Betty, once the most powerful and highest-paid star in Hollywood—the first woman to achieve #1 box-office status—left the motion picture industry in the shadow of Marilyn Monroe's rising star. America was changing, and with it our conceptions of women and sexuality. Betty would go on as a regular in the Las Vegas clubs and eventually to New York as Broadway's favorite Dolly—a role that was in many ways the high point of her career. Today, Betty's star still shines. Her pin-up lives on as a pop icon of patriotism, a living symbol of all that is good about America.

Tropicana Golf Course. It would be groovy to Have you stay with me. I've still got Puppy and Monty [her pet dogs]. Puppy's now 12 and Monty 10. I thought I was tied down a little when Vicki and Jess were still Home, but you know us with dogs . . .

Harry Has a new baby boy. I can't figure out what our grandchildren are to it in relationship, but it is wild, isn't it? Jessie, I guess I told you Has a girl and a boy and Vicki, a boy. They're both very Happy. Thank God. So I go on my own little way and I guess everything is about as good as could be expected. You sounded Happy which you know means a lot to me. Do you think we'll ever make that trip we've talked about in our old, old age? I'm old now, so we best not wait too long. I think so often of the things we used to get into.

I went to Del Mar for a couple of days last week and that really brought back memories. It's not the same anymore, but for God's sake—it's been twenty-one years!

Well, Honey, I'll say bye for now, and remember, I'll always love you and you'll always be my very, very best girlfriend.

Love,

Betty

"Unfortunately," Jessie says, "I don't think Michael was my father's son. You see, Joan Boyd was just one of those menopausal-men things and unfortunately she took him for a ride . . . I think she was sharp enough to figure out 'Here's a good one—latch on to this one, get the trust fund for the kid' kind of thing."

When James tired of his wife, he moved back to the bachelor quarters he shared with Phil Harris and began turning to Betty for money again. Jessie, however, became heavily influenced by her stepmother and moved with her children into Joan's apartment, where Joan had Michael, Jessie's stepbrother. Harry told Betty the two women and their children lived in deplorable conditions: unmade beds, cigarette butts, empty liquor bottles strewn about—and degenerates all over the place. Jessie now denies she ever lived with Joan. But Betty Ritz recalled that Grable on several occasions expressed grave concerns for Jessie's welfare.

"Oh, if only she would talk to me," Betty said to Jeff Parker.

"Why can't she talk to me? I'm her mother, for God's sake. Let her go and do that [referring to Jessie's problems] but *why* won't she talk to me?"

Joan introduced Jessie to the kinkier side of Vegas. Jessie recalls, "Joan was being real weird and she had all these weird people over there—real kinky. I wasn't into that. Especially not in my father's house, anyhow." One night Joan arranged a date between Jessie and Elvis Presley. "That was weird, too. I didn't like him. I liked the bartender instead. So I went up there that night to meet Elvis. There were some other women there, too. I thought he was gross. I didn't like him at all so I went over and talked to this cute bartender. Elvis got mad and stormed back into his rooms. The bartender and I left together."

Aunt Marjorie, too, recalled how the relationship between Jessie and Joan worried Betty. "Oh yes, Joan and Jessie got very close. I understood. It wasn't good for either of them . . . I don't like Joan."

Jessie compared herself with her mother in one respect. Betty had always disdained celebrities, and now Jessie chose the company of "real people," as her mother always referred to them. "The people who I hung out with," Jessie relates, "were porters and maids in the bathrooms—you know, the people that clean up, because they were the 'real people.'"

After Joan and Harry legally separated, accusations flew back and forth. Jessie had to stop seeing Joan because "my father would have real hard feelings toward me if he knew I was in cahoots with Joan." The last time Jessie visited Joan, she was very much aware of the significant personality changes in little Michael. Joan gave Jessie $200 to purchase a used car, and Jessie admits she never paid it back.

Harry's business manager, Pee Wee Monte, advised him to fight the demands Joan asked for in the divorce settlement. She was finally granted token support and a $30,000 trust fund for Michael, to be given to him when he turned twenty-one.

Today Joan's and Michael's whereabouts are unknown to Jessie. "She may be living on a houseboat or trailer somewhere, for all I know," Jessie says, "but Pee Wee Monte knows where she is."

Despite all the chaos surrounding her, Betty continued to express her devotion to Harry. Betty Ritz said, "I think she loved him because—she loved him. You can't tell why somebody loves somebody. But I think that you also love a talent. And Harry James, to me, and I think to her, was one of the greatest talents in the world."

As if to complete the ravaging of Betty's life, Billie died and Betty had a major falling-out with Marjorie. Divorced from Harry, estranged from her daughters and her sister, Betty Grable pulled herself together and headed East to rehearse for the Vegas production of *Hello, Dolly!*

# CHAPTER 16

Jerry Herman, Tony Award–winning composer and lyricist, had idolized Betty Grable since he was a teenager, plastering his bedroom walls with dozens of her photographs. "I can't tell you how it felt knowing this woman was singing for me," he said. "I had grown up in awe of her. That was just incredible for me. She was very frightened through the whole rehearsal period. The rehearsals *were not fun!* She was a very scared little lady but we all encouraged her and she was treated very well."

*Hello, Dolly!* was originally written for Ethel Merman, who turned it down for retirement. In time Merman would be one of a series of nine stars who helped keep the show running on Broadway for seven years. It opened on Broadway with Carol Channing as Dolly Levi the matchmaker.

"We all tried to find ladies who had their own aura," Jerry Herman said, "stars who could bring something special to the role. We took Ginger Rogers, obviously a symbol of a bygone era, just for that reason; and Ethel Merman for that reason—

she's Miss Show Business as far as I'm concerned. And then we put Mary Martin into it on the road because Mary loves to travel and, besides, she's a big star. I don't remember who first mentioned Betty Grable for the part. But I remember my reaction of 'Wow, that would be great!'

"Betty was probably one of *the* five movie stars. There was Lana Turner, Rita Hayworth, Elizabeth Taylor—and you know, one or two others."

Betty was first considered for *Dolly* when Eddie Fisher, during a performance at the Riviera Hotel in Las Vegas, stopped the show to introduce Betty, who was with Vicki and her husband. Fisher said Betty should be the next Dolly and the audience roared its approval. The management contacted producer David Merrick, who in turn called Betty.

Jerry Herman found nothing remarkable about the fact that so many different stars, including Phyllis Diller, Eve Arden, Martha Raye, Bibi Osterwald, and Pearl Bailey, could play Dolly Levi. "I mean, I could have put my grandmother in there and it would have run on its own momentum because it was so successful.

"The role of Dolly is written like a big lovable cartoon character that almost anybody can make their own. I'm not saying it was as good with Betty Grable—because it wasn't. And remember, I loved the lady and I wish I didn't have to say that . . . Besides, she would appreciate [it]. It wasn't as good with her as it was with—I just don't want to get into personalities because I loved them all—or at least most of them. However, Barbra Streisand was wildly wrong in the film version. Because she was only twenty-four *[sic]* years old playing the part of a sixty-year-old woman who has one more chance—before the parade passes by—and that's what that show's all about. It is about a woman who has one more chance."

Betty's Las Vegas production of *Dolly* opened as an immediate success. At the opening-night party she was photographed with her number-one fan, Carol Burnett. Burnett publicly invited Grable to join her in forming an act at the end of the run, but Grable, thanks to her enormous drawing power, would stay with the show for sixteen months. Betty did appear on

Burnett's television comedy show and became the first star to get Merrick's permission to sing "Hello, Dolly" on television.

When Louis Armstrong, who had a hit record of the song, came to Vegas during Betty's run, he asked to appear on stage with her, where he belted out a reprieve. A photograph of that moment, with Betty in costume and looking adoringly at "Satchmo," would be the only show-business memento permitted in her home.

Betty's best moment in the show, according to Jerry Herman: the moment she stood alone on a darkened stage, said, "Hey, what about me?" and then sang her heart out with "Before the Parade Passes By."

"She was so vulnerable," Herman said. "It was that vulnerability that was her greatest asset. She was a softy and you could tell this was a woman who could be very hurt if her lover ran off.

"Now I'm going to tell you the truth. Betty Grable sang fairly well; Betty Grable danced fairly well; and Betty Grable acted fairly well. But put it all together with that face and body—and those legs—and it became simply wonderful. *That's* what makes a star . . . And I'm sure *she* didn't know why she was a star."

Although miked to accommodate her limited vocal powers, on opening night Betty literally stopped the show in the scene in which Dolly invokes the spirit of her dead husband.

Ginger Rogers proved to be one of the most temperamental and uncooperative of all the Dollys in the original Vegas production. Though her contract with Merrick clearly spelled out an obligation to appear twice nightly, seven days a week, Rogers balked and later claimed she couldn't bear the smoking and gambling of the hotel show room. Merrick brought in Dorothy Lamour as an alternate replacement but her lackluster interpretation soon ended all of Merrick's hopes for a successful Vegas run. It was Grable, a second thought really, who finally revived and saved the show. It went on to break all records for a Vegas theatrical production.

Barbra Streisand came to see Betty's *Dolly* in Las Vegas. She was in the earliest stages of preparation for her $16 million–flop film of the musical. Streisand was struck by the amount of effort it took for Betty to get through the performance, and she came away from *Dolly* wondering aloud to her company why Grable ever subjected herself to such an obviously taxing situation. Barbra did not go backstage, though it would have thrilled Betty. When Betty saw *Funny Girl* staged in New York, she was so impressed with Barbra that she personally selected a dozen long-stem roses and sent them to her dressing room.

Betty worked every night for nine months straight in period costumes, makeup, and wigs. The work began to take its toll on her physically. She believed the wigs were responsible for her increasing hair loss. Between shows she could barely muster her voice above a whisper as she lay prostrate on her dressing room divan, perspiration oozing from under her heavy costume. Often she had a burning fever, but she refused to see a doctor. Photographer John Engstead recounted, "A call came asking if I could do a few rush pictures of Betty Grable that very day. The only time I had available was after work. So Betty came in that night about six. She wore no makeup and had none with her, although at that point in her career she needed a little help. I found some makeup and lashes and she left the application completely up to me. It was difficult to believe that after all these years Betty had never learned how to fix her face. An actress needs to know how to put on makeup, just as a plumber needs to know how to clean out a drain."

"I'd go with it to Africa," Betty proclaimed. "I'm absolutely in love with the role of Dolly Levi and the whole company. When I go on stage my tensions and anxieties just fade away. The show actually brings me happiness."

Betty was attracted to a young dancer in the company, Bob Remick, who was known as something of a stallion among the girls of the cast. Just as a male star might woo a pretty girl in the chorus, Betty courted Bob Remick, squiring him around town to supper clubs and showering him with lavish gifts, including a fur coat. Blond, blue-eyed, and stockily built, the five-foot ten-inch Brooklyn-born dancer soon quit show business at Betty's command and became her live-in companion and confidant. Betty expected Remick to do everything for her, and she was quick to berate him, even in public or in front of her entourage. She expected him to run *all* her errands—like buying makeup, making phone calls, arranging reservations, and mailing letters.

Bob Isoz first met Betty after a nightclub performance at the Latin Quarter in New York. Eventually Isoz, along with Mikey Levitt and Len Scumaci of Chicago, became weekend houseguests in Las Vegas. Levitt recalled that Betty was still terrified of sleeping alone. He was at Betty's Vegas house the night she had an altercation with Remick. The quarrel became so heated Remick walked out. When he failed to return by bedtime, Grable bid Mikey good night and they retired to their bedrooms. In the dark house, with storm winds howling across the desert, Betty panicked. She gently opened Mikey's bedroom door and crawled into bed with him. In the morning, Mikey asked her about her midnight visit. She smiled and shrugged her shoulders.

"Bob Remick was her handyman," Isoz recalled, "a gofer, and would go, for her, anywhere." Once when the three were riding in an elevator Betty angrily demanded to know why Remick had failed to mail letters to her fans. "She got mad at him a lot," Isoz added.

Unlike Betty, who continued to maintain her early morning "studio" schedule, Remick liked to sleep late. Though they shared an enthusiasm for alcohol, Betty often criticized Remick for his tendency to put on weight and his "slovenly ways." She would call him "Fatso" when she was angry with him, which was almost all the time.

Jerry Herman believes that, despite their problems together, Remick was a good match for Betty. "I think she grabbed on to somebody who paid attention to her and he was very nice to her in his own way. He was in love with her too, and we all appreciated that. I thought that odd as it might have been to some people, the age difference, it was a very successful relationship. And that's all we cared about. Somebody was making her happy. She would have been a much lonelier lady without Remick. Though I think she would have latched on to someone else if it were not for him."

After Betty and Bob Remick visited Betty Ritz in Mexico, Grable wrote a thank-you letter in which she offered her views on Bob: "He is dependable, loyal and a good companion; though I wish he would leave me and find a woman closer in age to him." Betty really never wished any such thing. She had become completely dependent on Remick and Remick belonged to her. A director working with Betty in the *Dolly* road company said, "He was a saint. Nobody treated Grable better than he did . . . He was the cutest thing you ever saw. He was gay and he was making it with another kid in the company on the sly. The poor kid got screwed up."

At parties they attended together, Betty was fiercely jealous when anyone flirted with Remick. "Lay off, sweetheart," she said to a shocked chorus girl who'd danced too long with Remick. The girl stormed across the room, turned, and glared at Grable. Betty stood her ground. Clutching her vodka, a cigarette dangling from parched lips, she stared the chorine down. Most of the leggy chorus girls knew better than to cross the aging movie queen. There were other problems with Remick; while Betty was off gambling, Remick spent the afternoons photographing beautiful models and showgirls in Betty's bedroom.

Betty Ritz, Mikey Levitt, and other friends have spoken of Grable's increasing jealousy and possessiveness. At Thanksgiving 1972 they were all Grable's houseguests, but Grable, resentful of Mikey's longtime lover, Ron, made it clear Ron was not to be invited. To resolve the uncomfortable situation, Ron stayed in a hotel on the Strip.

After Thanksgiving dinner, Mikey invited everyone to a midnight lounge show. When Grable declined, Mikey, seeing a chance to escape Grable's foul temper for a few hours, offered to take Betty Ritz and Ron. "I don't care if you go," Grable snapped. "Go on—go on—I could care less!"

"We'll be back soon," Mikey promised.

"Well, you know something," she muttered petulantly, "I don't care if you ever come back."

Betty Ritz took Mikey aside and advised, "I better not go. You two go ahead—and God, have the time of your life."

After the show Mikey and Ron returned to the house to find Grable and Ritz had had a few drinks. Betty pulled a complete reversal in her attitude toward the pair by jumping up and welcoming Ron effusively while ignoring Mikey completely. "Yes, Betty was very possessive," Mikey remembered.

In October 1965 Betty was summoned to New York to face one of her greatest challenges—playing Dolly Levi before the tough Manhattan legitimate-theater audience and the even tougher Broadway critics.

# CHAPTER 17

After Carol Channing passed the *Hello, Dolly!* mantle to her replacement, Ginger Rogers, it became customary for each new Dolly to pay a courtesy call on the outgoing star. Betty now steeled herself for a mandatory visit with Ginger, who had been holding forth at the St. James for months. Betty's antipathy toward Ginger dated back to 1934, when Betty had appeared in the chorus of *The Gay Divorcee;* Rogers, the star, had seemed arrogant to Betty and the other chorus girls. Betty attended a performance of Ginger's *Dolly* and headed backstage with a companion during intermission.

"I understand you're going to *replace* me when I go on my vacation," Ginger said.

"Oh no, I'm not," Grable replied. "I'm going on vacation to get rid of this throat." Betty referred to a hoarseness she had developed and had neglected to have checked by a doctor.

Neither star bothered to fill up the tense moments that followed. Instead Grable signaled to her companion it was time to leave for the second act. At the show's conclusion, Rogers stepped forth to speak, asking for the spotlight to shine on Betty Grable as planned. The audience craned their necks in vain as the spotlight illuminated an empty seat. Grable had bolted the instant Rogers started to speak. Fearing another jab, she had fled the St. James.

Betty was returning to Broadway for the first time since her triumph in *Du Barry Was a Lady*. On her opening night as Dolly, the customary sophisticated New York audiences went wild. It required six mounted policemen to clear a path for Betty as she left the St. James Theater after the performance.

"Betty Grable was the best received 'Dolly' of them all," a critic for the *New York Post* wrote, referring to Betty's four standing ovations. Discussing the audience's demonstration, the *New York Times* critic Vincent Canby wrote, "There was hardly a dry eye in the house as the audience, according to the lyrics, welcomed her back to where she belongs . . . [The audience gave] an extraordinary performance by any standard, noisy, hysterical, charged with emotion, a performance that was rooted in the effulgent memories of *Down Argentine Way* and *Moon Over Miami*. Behind it, one suspects, there was a lament for youth forever lost. That, however, was the performance of the St. James Theatre audience, at least, of a demonstrative minority of the audience, and it bore little relation to what happened on stage."

Canby added, "At fifty, Miss Grable looks great. The dimples in the Pretty Girl are intact. The outlines of the Pretty Girl figure have filled in a bit—those appendages that Dad used to call gams are still magnificent from the occasional glimpses we get beneath the turn-of-the-century gowns.

"Dolly, which has been pushed to fit the shapes and talents of all sorts of leading ladies, is in competent hands. It is not, however, in the hands of a sort of Queen of Camp, which is what you might have suspected if you had heard the audience Monday night. There was a very special clique that greeted Miss Grable's pleasantly conventional approach to comedy as if she were really Mae West, that responded to her sweet, breathy singing of Jerry Herman's lyrics as if Maria Callas had gone through the roof.

"This is only worth mentioning because it is a disservice to the star, who was playing it straight true to her fashion.

"Miss Grable's Dolly Levi lacks a certain free-wheeling wackiness and the kind of incredible dominating self-assurance that would make the farce as funny as it is frantic. Thus the high comic moments of this version are left almost entirely to the subsidiary characters."

Such a reception in New York would normally open up a score of creative possibilities for a new career, and her amicable relationship with Harry James should have put to rest most of Betty's problems—but neither of these came true. As she grew more confident in her new status as a Broadway star, Grable plunged into conflict with producer David Merrick. It was 20th Century–Fox all over again. Her insecurities and paranoia fully reactivated, the star victimized and attacked members of the wardrobe and makeup departments—only now she accused them of stealing a number of her personal items. This may have been a devious ploy to keep them out of her dressing room while she imbibed her vodka. Whatever the case, Grable's behavior presented problems to the management and staff responsible for the smooth unfolding of a show with split-second production cues.

David Merrick always made a point of visiting his Dollys on a regular basis, ostensibly to resolve any problems they had with the production. But in Betty's case he did not provide the same service. When she toured with the show in Washington, D.C., Grable reached into her bag of old studio tricks and took her case to the press. "I got sick one night and couldn't go on," she told a reporter, "and David Merrick threatened to bring me up on charges before Equity. I thought, 'Gee, that's great. I'll have to fly to New York to answer the charges and that will give me a day off.' The same thing must have occurred to Merrick, because he dropped the charges."

Merrick never replied, realizing, perhaps, that a rebuttal could be used against him at the box office—where it hurts. He knew, as Grable knew, that the star drew the audience.

The nation's critics, during her national tour with *Dolly,* were charmed by Betty and the nostalgic associations she generated.

But they shared the opinion that her Dolly wasn't imbued with the brassy busybody qualities the role called for. The press for the tour reveals the critics had a common complaint about her voice, whether it was because of her hoarseness or insufficient audibility.

"The Grable voice had more sighs where Carol Channing had more volume and just plain gravel. But her songs were well presented by her sheer force of personality," wrote Mary M. Jordan, of a Scranton, Pennsylvania, newspaper. Roger Dittmer of a Chicago paper wrote: "Miss Grable—in spite of a cold that inhibited her singing last night—cavorted on famously." R. P. Harris of the Baltimore *News-America* noted: "As Dolly, Miss Grable's opulent charms and her valiant efforts to cope with a voice problem quickly won a sympathetic audience."

"Bad sound and probably a bit of laryngitis couldn't stop Betty Grable from being a garrulous, charming, philosophical, conniving Dolly Gallagher Levi," wrote Frank G. Schmidt of the *South Bend Tribune.*

Her director believed Betty's chronic hoarseness came on because "she didn't know how to project onstage." But even offstage at that time, Betty sometimes found it difficult to be understood. She was smoking three packs of cigarettes a day.

Ralph Pearl was almost fired from his "Vegas Daze and Nites" column in the *Las Vegas Sun* because of some remarks he made about Betty in *Hello, Dolly!* Betty claimed in private that Pearl's attack was provoked by her refusal to respond to his sexual advances. There was a public outcry. The Riviera Hotel, where *Dolly* was staged, protested, and Pearl was forced to apologize. But he was one of the first to detect Betty's chronic case of laryngitis. "Betty Grable," he wrote, "is still fighting a bad case of laryngitis, still making with the 'show must go on' bit at the Riviera."

A *Fort Worth Star-Telegram* critic wrote Betty was "battling a hoarseness that ironically was brought on in San Antonio when she had to sing louder because of another balky mike . . ."

Betty's health problems began after her divorce, after Jessie left home, and after Billie died. All her support systems had collapsed. Why she waited so long to visit a doctor is probably attributable to her hatred and distrust of the medical profession and the attendants who had let her father die in admissions.

Betty returned home to Las Vegas with Bob Remick. She began accepting offers to appear in road companies of other Broadway hits—*High Button Shoes, Guys and Dolls,* and *Plaza Suite.* Her old friend and former costar Rory Calhoun, now a stage producer, offered Grable the starring role in a new musical, *Belle Starr,* set to open in London's West End. The material was developed from an original Las Vegas floor show and the 1941 Gene Tierney–Randolph Scott movie Western of the same title. Convinced she had at last found a theatrical property she could originate, Betty foresaw a major breakthrough for her career. Despite the disastrous *Beautiful Blonde From Bashful Bend,* Betty still clung to the idea that a gunslinging turn-of-the-century adventuress could do for her what *The Unsinkable Molly Brown* had done for Tammy Grimes. Betty excitedly prepared for her first trip abroad.

The pre-London opening was in Glasgow. Though the Scottish press and audiences were delighted by her, the show was a total loss; the book, songs, and staging were uniformly wretched. Although the nightly recipient of ovations and flowers, Betty sensed a calamity in the making.

Marjorie—to whom Betty had not spoken since Billie's death—phoned from Los Angeles to say that Betty's photo was being splashed across the front pages of U.S. newspapers. Actress Lita Baron Calhoun, Rory Calhoun's wife, had named Betty as one of ninety-three adulterous corespondents in her divorce complaint against Rory. Betty had been singled out by the press because of her celebrity status. In private she cracked, "At least I could or should have been third on the list. The closest I ever got to Rory was when he pulled out a chair for me to sit on at his daughter's birthday party."

Around the corner in the West End, Grable's old nemesis Ginger Rogers was starring in Jerry Herman's London production of *Mame.* The press noted the two stars' clashing styles as they arrived in London—Grable, sedate; Rogers, flamboyant.

Veronica Lake, another blonde survivor of forties stardom, was also performing in London.

Reporters ignored the Rory Calhoun scandal as they swarmed around Betty during her first London press conference. Looking drawn and tired, Betty sat stiffly on a straight-back chair, wearing a short black dress and ballerina shoes. She nervously crossed and recrossed her legs, brushed at faded strands of hair slipping from under her blond wig. Chain-smoking and hoarse as she chatted with the press, Grable said London was like "a dream come true." She went on, "I never bothered to look at my movies after I finished them—but if I had to pick one I'd have to say I like *The Dolly Sisters* [she incorrectly identified Dan Dailey as her costar]. He was one of my favorite leading men." She admitted she smoked too much, puffing away with a blank look. "I once said I'm not pretty enough to be a dramatic star, and I can't act, and what the public expects from me is a flashy wardrobe, plenty of makeup and false eyelashes—" The reporters gasped at Betty Grable's self-deprecating attitude. She added: "That's not quite true. I suppose you can say today that I am offering memories . . . and if it hadn't been for my mother I would never have become a movie star."

Exhausted, Betty canceled subsequent interviews and personal appearances. Though the show opened on April 30, 1969, a May Day strike of newspaper workers silenced the critics until May 3, when Betty awoke to discover the critics had blasted her London debut.

Betty pointed out the British audiences were "wonderful" and that, after all, was what really mattered. "In my entire career, I don't remember any of my movies getting a good review."

To reporters who mentioned her hoarseness, she said, "I have strained my throat but if I started worrying about that I better quit and go home. You know," she added, irrelevantly, inaccurately, and poignantly, "I've never had my heart broken—and I hope it doesn't happen."

"Miss Grable's legs are well-matched, pretty and able to

dance effortlessly for several seconds at a time," remarked a scathing critic.

As a Western saloon madam, Grable yelled nightly, "She's got the biggest pair of 38s in town," shimmying across the stage in a gold lamé cowgirl suit, skirt slit to the waist, brandishing a pair of six-shooters.

Bette Davis was in the audience one night and sent an encouraging note to Grable backstage. Betty was deeply grateful and met briefly with Davis after the show.

Ross Petty, a featured singer in the show, said, "I found her helpless, buffeted by all the people around her and not really knowing what was going on." Petty felt this was one time that her personality was unable to save a poor performance. "You wonder how somebody who doesn't believe in themselves can make it."

As soon as the show was recognized as an unmitigated disaster, producer Calhoun and his partner disappeared. When Betty learned they'd left town without paying the members of the chorus their last week's salary, she quietly footed the bill, perhaps an unprecedented gesture in the annals of the theater. Betty herself was never paid—though she had borne some of the producers' expenses, including the additional, though mediocre, Steve Allen material commissioned to punch up a miserable score, and extra costumes Grable had deemed essential.

"I haven't been paid yet," she said to a reporter, "but I am told it is being held for me while the tax position is worked out." In the U.S., Actors' Equity would never have permitted such shabby treatment of a performer. Grable had gambled and lost. *Belle Starr* closed after twenty-one performances.

Betty's childhood friend Paula Stone lived in London and they met several times. Paula said Betty seemed drastically changed—she was aging radically and appeared broken and preoccupied, she was not the fun-loving, exuberant Betty Paula remembered from fifteen years before. Paula was particularly struck by Betty's bullying of Bob Remick, who never uttered a word of protest and remained steadfastly obedient and attentive.

Betty did not discuss with Paula the problems tearing at her—the divorce, the strained relationship with Jessie, or even Billie's death. "She locked it all up inside," Paula said, "and now I'm terribly sorry that she did . . . She always did that when she was very unhappy—just as she had been about Artie Shaw."

Paula saw Betty and Bob off on an ocean liner bound for home. Looking exhausted and depressed, Betty clung desperately to Paula as she said goodbye. It was the last time she was ever to see her childhood girlfriend.

# CHAPTER 18

Dorothy Lamour and Betty Grable were devoted to each other and often exchanged expensive gifts, though Lamour could never match her friend's extravagant generosity. Dorothy finally asked Betty to agree *not* to exchange further gifts, but Betty continued to express her appreciation for Lamour's loyalty by lavishing presents on her anyway. She was oddly reluctant, however, to spend time with Dorothy or other women friends who sought her out.

In 1971 Lamour and Grable appeared together in a St. Louis summer theater revue, *That's Show Business.* A perfect chance to spend some time together socially, Lamour thought. But every time she proposed dinner, Betty graciously turned her down to scamper off with Bob Remick and Mikey Levitt. Several months later, Betty received a birthday present from Dorothy—a hand-made hooked rug in her favorite colors, similar to one she had admired backstage in St. Louis. Betty responded by sending her an expensive blouse Dorothy still treasures.

When visiting Las Vegas, Dorothy would phone Betty, who

always begged off with a lame excuse. Chita Rivera, who appeared in the same St. Louis revue, also found Betty stand-offish. Once, to Mikey Levitt, she said: "I wish she'd let me be her friend."

Alice Faye remembered, "Betty and I were never close. We worked together—you know what I mean? We got closer, not really that close, when we retired. She was a beautiful lady, lots of fun, and she certainly loved life." One evening in Vegas Betty and Alice sat on the patio, gazing up at a star-filled desert sky. "Wouldn't it be wonderful," Grable said, sipping her drink, "if we just got up and started singing all the old songs? You know, out here on the patio, keeping all the neighbors up?"

Carol Burnett remembers the first time she met Grable, her childhood idol, when Betty arrived for rehearsals for an appearance on *The Carol Burnett Show.*

"She was just so easygoing. She came in with no agents or managers—just alone, you know—and she came up to the office for a reading. Martha Raye was on the show that week, too.

"Well, between the two of them I never said a word. I just laughed all week. Betty had a very laid-back sense of humor and you know Martha's is bombastic. Martha would have everybody rolling in the aisles and then Betty would just kind of lay back and then she'd say a line that would top everybody's."

Only on rare occasions, Jessie recalls, did her mother reveal her dry sense of humor—and only then if she initiated the fun. Any jokes or pranks the girls started were always met with icy silence as Betty dared them to go further. "My mother sometimes would poke fun at her 'million-dollar legs,'" Jessie says. "Mother said if they had really been insured for that amount she would have cut them off long ago."

Mikey Levitt remembers that Betty once sat back in her chair, hoisted her legs on the table, and cracked, "You little moneymakers. That one's worth half a mil and that one's worth half a mil."

Jessie comments, "My mother never had any control over

her life as a child; nor was she ever allowed to make any independent decisions. What kind of confidence are you going to have? Her mother made her what she was and so when your mother's not there when you're getting older—

"There was a lot of love there. She just didn't know how to express it. She really didn't want to hug and stuff like that. There just was not a lot of touching so that when there *was* touching, it was abnormal."

Her Vegas friends invariably described Betty as a fun-loving, sexy, saucy, wisecracking dame who enjoyed nothing more than turning the stage crews and chorus boys on with risqué jokes. Once, backstage, Grable knocked on the men's dressing room door and wiggled in, singing "Would You Like to Swing on a Star?" Executing some mean bumps and grinds, she playfully taunted the chorus boys, "How would you like to swing on *this* star?" Whenever asked what film during her long career was her very favorite, Grable would somewhat curiously refuse to answer the question. Then she would just as suddenly volunteer her own version of the titles: *Mother Wore Tights* became "Mother Was Tight"; *The Farmer Takes a Wife*, "The Farmer Takes a Dike"; and *Meet Me After the Show*, "Beat Me After the Show."

Travilla ran into Betty when she brought his design collection to Vegas. Shortly after he entered the dress shop at the Desert Inn, a saleslady told him, "Mr. Travilla, in Dressing Room A is a tired old showgirl that wants to say hello." In Dressing Room A, it turned out, was Betty Grable, "looking wonderful," Travilla says. "She was suntanned and her hair was pulled back in a little ponytail—cute figure, just looking great—and that was the last time I saw her. Betty had a lot of love for the people she liked—but she was also full of hate for the world."

Betty and Bob were always quarreling. After a performance in southern Illinois one night, Betty learned Bob had made a date with another woman. She pushed Remick out of the car into the snow and drove off with Bob Isoz. At her hotel, Betty began scolding Isoz for not wearing snow boots. Increasingly edgy as she awaited Remick's return, Betty lashed out at Isoz again when he casually mentioned he had taken his son to an X-rated movie. Betty angrily admonished him: "Bob, how could you—you of all people—do such a terrible thing?"

In St. Louis Mikey Levitt joined Betty and Remick in the middle of a fight. Returning to her hotel room, Betty slipped in before the two men and slammed the door in their faces. The men retired to a bar. When they returned to the hotel, Betty was in the lounge, drunk and seething with anger. With one shoe on and one shoe off, and only one false eyelash in place, she said, "Hey, Fatso," pointing to Remick, "where the hell have you been?" They helped her back to her room, but Grable again managed to slip in and lock them out. The two men took another hotel room, where they spent the night together. The next morning Betty accused them of having had an affair, which was of course not true.

Mikey tolerated these outbursts as he, along with Remick, assumed protective custody of Betty. Whenever she went over the edge with her drinking or gambling, Levitt and Remick tried to stay by her side. One night when Betty urged them to join her for a few hours of gambling, they made her promise not to take along more than $200. This she promptly lost and then produced another $400 "from out of a glove, or under a bracelet or behind an earring." When Grable started winning, the men stealthily withdrew $400 of chips from her pile. She then went on to lose everything and admitted on the way home even the $400 she had smuggled out of the house was lost.

When they settled into the living room, the men proudly brought forth the $400 they had managed to extricate. Instead of being grateful, Betty began to curse them, her face turning crimson. She snatched the money from their hands, tore each bill to shreds, dashed into the bathroom, and flushed the money down the toilet. Another night of horror.

When she gambled, Grable was ruled by a number of superstitions. She believed she could alter her luck if she rubbed the dice or blew on them, changed her seat, used good-luck charms, or changed the deck of cards. Sometimes she prayed a dealt card or a roll of the dice would favor her.

Betty Grable was a nest of neurotic superstitions. In *The Beau-*

*tiful Blonde from Bashful Bend,* she yelled when Conchita, played by Olga San Juan, put a hat on the bed. The episode reflected a real-life phobia. She had a horror of hats, shoes, and umbrellas on beds and never permitted hats on closet shelves. These were terrible omens. "Take those hats down from that closet shelf," she once told Harry. "Don't ever put those shoes over your head. Because it's bad luck." Betty always put her left shoe on before the right. Shoes held remarkable powers. If a pair ever ended up on a table, Grable threw them out. Those shoes were "set on the long march of the dead into the underworld."

Friends never wished Grable good luck. Good luck was bad luck. One did not whistle in her dressing room or take anything from her hand.

Superstitions appealed strongly to Betty's irrational side. Since she had received no spiritual guidance from her mother, they helped allay her many fears. Crowds horrified Grable, and her refusal to attend important film events infuriated studios for decades.

She believed in ghosts and spoke of them in wide-eyed whispers. "She often heard ghosts creeping around the upstairs bedroom," Marjorie said, "and she really believed that she shared some kind of mysterious and special bond with them."

When Carol Burnett bought Betty's Los Angeles house, since demolished, Betty asked if Carol had heard "the ghosts," and Carol laughed, assuming her friend was joking. Betty went along with it, calling them "ghosties" and dismissing the subject with a quip, "I always thought it was my ol' Harry clunking around upstairs."

Carol remembered, "The house when I bought it was reported to have little ghosties in it—English ghosties. I think the bricks for that Doheny house were brought over from England and taken from an old castle. Remember the movie *The Ghost Goes West*? A lot of those castle bricks used in that film were eventually used for the house—and the ghosties came with it."

A firm believer in the occult, Betty studied numerology. The total number of letters in the name Betty Grable is eleven. The two digits in 11 add together to equal 2—Grable's number. Her full name can also be reduced down to 2: Elizabeth Ruth "Betty" Grable James equals 29—2 + 9 = 11; 1 + 1 = 2. As one of two daughters, she became the mother of two daughters and married twice—once to Coogan for two years, and later to Harry for twenty-two years. Even her home addresses had numbers divisible by two: 3858 Lafayette Street in St. Louis, 1280 Stone Canyon and 600 Doheny Road in Los Angeles, and 164 Tropicana Road in Las Vegas.

Another approach numerologists use in determining a person's number is the date of birth, the 18th for Grable: 1 + 8 = 9. Persons born with the number 9 have a difficult childhood, which they overcome in maturity. They develop into strong-willed fighters who are determined, impulsive, and quick-tempered and who strive to be their own masters. Their home life is filled with strife and quarreling.

On the positive side for 9s, they are excellent organizers when given absolute control. Loss of control triggers loss of heart; they stand aside and let things fall apart. They do not ask for a peaceful or monotonous life. Certainly 9 was Betty's number.

# CHAPTER 19

Harry James and Phil Harris were appearing together at the Frontier Hotel. Betty went for a visit one night, accompanied by Bob Remick. Alice Faye joined them and the group assembled in a trailer dressing room behind the hotel for an evening of drinking and swapping stories.

Dancer Jeff Parker was also invited. "They were all there," Parker remembered. "Betty told a story about some celebrity she knew who couldn't walk very gracefully." She rose from the couch to demonstrate and began to wobble from the effects of the alcohol. "Of course I don't walk too well either," she confessed, breaking up everyone present.

Parker asked Betty about a favorite movie of his, *Billy Rose's Diamond Horseshoe*. She shook her head solemnly and protested, "Don't date us, baby—please, don't date us."

Later that night, after leaving the group, Parker said Betty turned morose. Drunk, she sobbed as she spoke about her divorce from Harry. Richard Allan says, "Betty told me that after the divorce she and Harry were better friends than when they were married. I've surmised that the divorce was because Harry at that age wanted something different—something newer and younger. She didn't want the divorce. I know, too, that Alice Faye pretends she and Phil Harris are happily married. But they're not."

Betty began seeing Harry without taking Remick along. They dined in a remote corner of her favorite Italian restaurant, Battista's, near the Las Vegas Riviera Hotel, where she was performing. Immaculately groomed and attentive, Betty was overheard responding to something Harry had said with, "Oh yes, Mr. James." She agreed to bail Harry out of his gambling debts with the money she earned from *Dolly*. These loans amounted to $1–1.5 million and were never repaid. Bob Remick still has the IOUs Harry signed to Betty. She never asked Harry to repay her, though she often blurted out in private she wished he would so she could pay her own gambling debts. Yet despite all the financial abuses, she readily accepted Harry's renewed interest in their relationship even after his divorce from Joan Boyd. Though she knew what James really wanted from her—money, and more and more money—Betty allowed herself to be drawn into the charade.

The renewed friendship with Harry offered Betty little comfort; she was still haunted by memories of her mother and problems with Jessie. Before each show she filled her flask with vodka, sneaking drinks during and after performances. Jessie says, "I took off and once went to South Africa and I didn't tell anybody—just went. The kids went to their dad in Colorado and I went and stayed two months because of this guy. *I was going to make it down there.*"

About her other daughter, Betty told Bob Isoz, "I don't like the way William [her son-in-law] treats Vicki. He teases her and makes fun of her." Mikey Levitt recalled, "The Bivenses would visit Las Vegas only when William won a free trip for his auto sales as a salesman for Chrysler. Betty would complain bitterly how they never stayed with her—opting instead for a hotel room. Betty loved her grandchildren but only because they were far away from her."

"She had the ism of alcoholism—lack of self-worth on one

hand and feelings of superiority on the other," said actor Jim Dybas, who worked with Betty. Only hours before she was to be honored at the 1972 Academy Awards ceremony, Betty started drinking, sitting in a restaurant with Bob Remick, Mikey Levitt, who had flown in from Chicago, and Bob Latin, a hairdresser Betty befriended during the run in *Hello, Dolly!* "I'm going to call and cancel," she was threatening when Mikey reached for the bread basket. Betty snatched up a roll and threw it at him. "What's the matter?" she snapped. "Can't you wait?"

After her triumph at the ceremony, broadcast worldwide on television, Betty and her entourage headed for a lavish party at the Beverly Wilshire. Peter Finch made his way through the celebrity-filled room, introduced himself, and sheepishly admitted he had always been an admirer. Betty returned the compliment.

Seated with Betty were Diane Baker and Martha Raye. Martha said the only reason she attended at all was that she had been told she would share a table with her "old friend Grable." Betty did not regard Martha as an old friend. In 1938, when Martha was the bigger star, they had indeed been friends. But when Betty eclipsed Martha, who slipped to featured secondary parts, the relationship grew strained. "Martha," Betty said, "just couldn't handle it." But Betty adored Ann Miller, who stopped by, snapped her gum, and cooed, "Hi, Doll. How ya doin'?" And Betty warmly embraced another old friend, Binnie Barnes.

Jack Nicholson sat at a table nearby. Betty considered him to be the sexiest man in films. She kept glancing his way, hoping to attract his attention with her shy little-girl glances and blushes. Twice during dinner she asked her companions if Nicholson was looking at her. He wasn't.

Jackie Coogan was there and although they did not meet, Betty criticized the Academy for failing to acknowledge Coogan's contributions as "The Kid" in the Chaplin film. Why, she wondered, did the Academy miss this rare chance to photograph the legendary pair, both present. Coogan visited Chaplin in his hotel suite the next day. When asked how it felt to see The Kid again, Chaplin said: "The Kid! That child. And then to see this bald-headed man who was sweet in those days . . ."

Martha Raye ordered another bottle of vodka for the table and everyone had a drink. Then, as she prepared to leave, Martha indicated that she wanted to put the bottle in her purse. "But later," Mikey recounted, "when the bill came, and after Martha had gone—and for that matter everyone else had gone except for Betty, Bob, and me—Betty paid for the vodka." Shaking her head and shrugging her shoulders, Grable commanded, "Come on, let's get the hell outta here."

"Something's terribly wrong," Grable moaned, doubled over from the second attack of pain in her abdomen since the flight back to Vegas from the Oscar ceremony. Again, Betty chose to ignore the problem.

She had always been indifferent to her health and, according to Betty Ritz, to any physical discomfort as well. Betty's chronic sniffles annoyed Ritz for years until finally one day she said, "Betty, why don't you blow your nose?"

"I have postnasal drip," Grable replied.

"Well, then blow—just blow your nose."

Ritz handed her a Kleenex. After using it, Grable beamed as if making a major discovery. From then on she often reminded Betty Ritz, "I never blew my nose until I met you. And now I can't stop blowing it."

Three weeks later, after a routine physical checkup required for her Australian tour of *No, No, Nanette,* Betty's Las Vegas physician asked her, "Do you have a doctor in Los Angeles?"

"Why, yes. We've had one for many years."

"Well, then," he advised, without going into detail, "I would suggest that you get in touch with him." He could not give her a final clearance until further tests were done on more sophisticated equipment.

Annoyed over having to return to Los Angeles, Betty checked into St. John's Hospital in Santa Monica, where a star-struck nurse asked if she might hang up Grable's negligee for her. "*What* negligee?" asked Betty, who hadn't even brought a suitcase.

"Don't you even have a hospital gown like the pretty ones they wear in the maternity ward?" the nurse persisted.

"Who do you think I am," Betty Grable said, "Joan Crawford?"

The tests were completed on the following day and Betty's doctor came to her room with a diagnosis. "I don't think you're going to make the trip to Australia, Miss Grable. I don't like what I've found on the X-rays we took of your lungs."

"Well, what is it? Is it cancer?"

"I'm afraid so."

Her worst fears now confirmed, her physician, Dr. Kositchek, assured her there was still hope, advising immediate exploratory surgery. On May 6, 1972, surgery was performed on Betty's neck to determine if the cancer spread to her lymph glands. It had. There was evidence of some metastasis; doctors administered cortisone and radium treatments during three weeks of hospitalization.

Bob Remick brought Betty back to Vegas. They were watching a television show one evening about a divorced middle-aged woman who was dying. Until then Betty had been stoic, but now she broke into hysterical disbelieving sobs, moaning she was going to die soon. "I can't do it! I can't do it! I can't do the Australia tour!" She phoned her agent and dropped out of the show.

"The *No, No, Nanette* production from Australia," announced *The New York Times,* "was to have starred Betty Grable, but she had to withdraw. She is being replaced by Cyd Charisse."

And there were other blows. Screen Actors Guild, to which Betty Grable had paid thousands of dollars in dues over the years, informed her that because of a technicality in its medical coverage any member not earning a minimum of $4,000 in films during the previous year was ineligible to collect benefits. (The minimum has since been amended to $2,400.)

With no one to turn to, not even Harry James, who still owed her over $1 million, Grable took the only course open to her. She went back to work. As she made plans for a return to the stage in *Born Yesterday,* Betty awoke one morning to discover her hair was falling out from the effects of cobalt and radium treatments. She took to drinking even more.

Bob Remick began a new career as a dealer at the MGM Grand Hotel Casino. Betty spent her lonely evenings in the company of gypsy chorus friends, appearing in the backup acts for Jane Powell and Debbie Reynolds, both of whom she deliberately avoided. Betty always found Debbie "too ballsy."

It was a heartbreaking sight—Betty Grable wobbling through the casinos on her way to the shows, stopping long enough to throw her money away on a few rolls of the dice and a couple of spins on the roulette wheel. Obviously she exceeded the maximum two drinks a day her physician allowed. She looked dazed from the combined effects of the cortisone and booze, her body disfigured by the bloating side effects of the drugs. As Grable set her chips out on the table, onlookers were struck by the swollen obliteration of her once flawlessly beautiful features, now framed by a cheap, dishwater-blond wig. Cigarette hanging from a gash-red mouth, Betty called out her losing bets in a husky voice now reaching a baritone pitch. Friends quietly shook their heads.

Jeff Parker was devastated at the sight of his friend and disturbed by her understandable sense of abandonment. "What can you do when you've got the Big C?" she asked. Grable bought a brown Mercedes she neither wanted nor could afford; Bob Remick, however, did want it.

By September, the cancer had quickly spread. Betty was readmitted to St. John's Hospital in Santa Monica, where she underwent more surgery. The disease had been arrested in the lungs but now invaded her intestines.

Leaving the hospital and driving to the Burbank airport for the flight to Vegas, Betty asked Bob to stop at a gay bar, The Hay Loft, where a Betty Grable film tribute was in progress. As she entered the darkened bar, her screen image was dancing on the wall. She boldly stepped in front of the projector. The patrons yelled in protest, then they recognized Betty Grable.

The lights came on as the men applauded and cheered. She hoisted herself onto the bar, exposed the still trim legs, crossed them, and proceeded to sign autographs for her fans.

Back in Vegas, Jeff Parker, who was working with Debbie Reynolds at the Desert Inn, arranged to have a screening of one of Betty's favorite films, *A Star Is Born* with Judy Garland, at her home. Betty loved Judy ever since they had worked together in *Pigskin Parade.* Attendants at the late-night soiree included Debbie Reynolds and her daughter, Carrie Fisher, Hollywood columnist Bob Osborne, Bob Remick, dancer Rudy Bender and his mother, and a number of other show-business people. Betty, though tired and weak, appreciated the warm gesture.

Word leaked to the press Betty was terminally ill. One report stated she had died and her body was secretly buried in an unmarked grave in Palm Springs. She blamed Rona Barrett and Rex Reed for keeping the rumors alive. On January 16, 1973, *Variety* managed to squelch most of the talk when they announced, "Happy to report that Betty Grable is A-OK. She's in Jacksonville, Florida, readying a January 23 start in *Born Yesterday* on an open date."

# CHAPTER 20

Bob Isoz visited Betty in Jacksonville, and after a performance of *Born Yesterday* they went to a restaurant. The show's two producers were already there, drinking and dining. As Betty and Isoz were being seated, Betty overheard the producers making salacious remarks about Isoz, who, they both agreed, was "hot." Grable stormed over to their table. With a hand on her hip she pointed her finger at them and said, "You lay off. He's a nice guy." She left her producers staring at each other in shock.

"I was really grateful to Betty that she would do that for me," said Isoz, who had felt his honor was at stake.

"Here I am doing *Born Yesterday*. I'm on the stage every night and they're writing—Rex Reed and Rona Barrett—that I'm dying. I'm fine," she lied to Bob. "Now how could I be dying if I'm doing this show?" But Betty also admitted that once onstage she found a curious relief from cancer pain by pouring her energy and concentration into the performance. By curtain she became so weak Bob Remick had to carry her from the stage to her dressing room. In one scene costar Art Kusel was required reluctantly to force her down on the sofa; this caused overwhelming pain in Betty's spine, despite Remick's daily injections of a powerful prescribed narcotic.

Back in Vegas, Betty Ritz visited Grable at the home of Toni Clark of the Desert Inn. After a few drinks, Grable took Ritz aside and untied the silk scarf she had carefully wrapped around her neck to disguise her surgical wounds. "Look what they did to me. Isn't that hell?"

The following morning, as the early winter sun filtered through the windows of Grable's sparsely furnished kitchen, Grable and Ritz sat and mused over cups of coffee. And as she spoke, unemotionally, of the hopelessness of her predicament, Grable picked up a Dunhill cigarette holder turned yellow from years of accumulated nicotine. Lighting her cigarette, her eyes misting, she said: "Now isn't that something? My mother always told me to use a cigarette holder when I smoked so I wouldn't get cancer—and here I have it. With the cigarette holder and filter and all." Unable to go on, Betty fought back tears and changed the subject.

"She was a great gal for livin'," Betty Ritz said, pointing out Grable had undergone a remarkable personality change and was trying very hard to be nice to everyone.

On April 24, 1973, a spokesman for St. John's Hospital announced Grable, fifty-six, was seriously ill with a duodenal ulcer. Her condition was improving, he said, but he added that further surgery seemed likely. Betty received hundreds of phone calls from well-wishers, but she preferred not to see visitors.

Among the few she did admit were her immediate family, Bob Remick, Mikey Levitt, Angie Blue, her old choreographer friend from Fox, and Alice Faye. Harry James never visited. When Mikey admired a bouquet Harry had sent, Betty said, "Well, I wish he'd send me some of the money he owes me instead."

On yet another visit Mikey was surprised to see her reading a book of prayers. "Mikey," she said sweetly, "I'm *really* sick today."

"Did you call for Brunhilda?" he asked, using Betty's nickname for her very German nurse.

"No," she said, flipping the book open to the first page, which June Haver had inscribed. "Nothing will help me now. June Haver came to visit this morning." She winked at Mikey and laughed.

Marjorie visited every day. The two sisters put aside all their differences. Now they sat chatting and playing cards. They had never been closer. One day Marjorie discovered Betty on her hands and knees, scrubbing the floor of her hospital room. Another time, while sliding out of bed, Betty unintentionally exposed her backside. The nurse said, "Now, Mrs. James, that's all right. Nobody's looking."

"Yeah?" Grable quipped. "Well, they used to."

On her twenty-sixth birthday, Jessie visited her mother. Betty took a hundred-dollar bill from her purse and tried to force it into her hand. "No, I can't take that," Jessie protested.

"Take it," Betty insisted. "I'm not going to be around for the next one. It's my money and I'll do what I want with it."

Jessie was surprised to learn that her mother had had a hysterectomy, and even until now she wonders why.

Dorothy Lamour spoke to Betty by phone every day. "Her spirits were high," Dorothy said, "and she wanted to get back to work. I was honored to be her friend. I only hope that some of her courage rubbed off on me."

Columnist Jim Bacon had known Betty well when she'd been with Ted Fio Rito. He received a note that said, "I'm feeling quite well now. I am resting and contemplating a return to work later on in the season." But Joyce Haber announced in the *Los Angeles Times* that Betty was gravely ill. "That bitch!" Dorothy Lamour lashed out, learning of Betty's distressed outburst when she'd read the Haber item. The news prompted a flood of phone calls to the hospital, tying up the switchboard for hours.

"Until I read the Haber item I thought I was recovering," Betty tearfully lied to reporters.

Alice Faye visited frequently, breaking out in cold sweats from the effort of finding appropriate words for her dying friend. Faye believed her visits were a great source of comfort to Betty. Whenever she prepared to leave, Betty always looked at her in tears and whispered, "I'll never see you again."

At last Betty was so heavily sedated she awoke only long enough to return a few personal phone calls or autograph a photo for a persistent fan. As word spread that Betty Grable was dying, bizarre things began to happen.

One fan whose license plate read GRABLE made a cross-country pilgrimage and was rewarded with the last autograph she would ever give. A scandal sheet offered Bob Remick $5,000 for a photo of Betty on her deathbed. Film historian Gene Ringgold beseeched President Nixon to provide a full military burial. "I was told," he later wrote, "that I was attempting something in bad taste, something that might conflict with family plans."

When the hospital could do nothing more for her, Betty was released and she returned to Vegas. Suffering a sudden turn for the worse, Grable realized Bob Remick could no longer handle the complicated nursing routine. She agreed to return to St. John's Hospital on the condition that she *not* be taken back by plane. Remick arranged to borrow a van, and, assisted by another fan, the three set out on a gruesome seven-hour drive under a scorching summer sun. Betty was down to seventy pounds. She wore a light-colored cotton bed robe and a white skullcap over her bald head—her "nigger cap," she called it. She lay stretched out in the back of the van as the bumps along the road intensified her agony.

The worn-out group finally reached Santa Monica, only to have an accident there. Remick, in a hurry to get Betty comfortably settled in a hospital bed, misjudged the maximum ceiling height of the emergency entrance and crushed the top of the van.

Remick phoned Marjorie to tell her Betty was back in St. John's. When Marjorie asked to speak to Betty, Remick hesitated to reveal her true physical state. He urged Marjorie to come to the hospital. "I walked in the room and walked right out," Marjorie said. "Bob hadn't warned me. Dr. Kositchek said that he was going to do one thing only for Betty—keep her comfortable."

Marjorie kept constant vigil over the shrunken form of her

sister. Jessie and Vicki came, and Mikey Levitt arrived from Chicago. "Oh, look," Betty whispered during a moment of consciousness. "Mikey is here—and he came on his own nickel."

On July 2, 1973, just before 5:00 P.M., Betty started struggling for breath. Remick rushed out to get Dr. Kositchek. By the time the two returned, Betty Grable was dead.

Within six hours Hollywood reeled from the news of Betty's death. Who will be the next? asked the regulars at Chasen's. Within the week Veronica Lake was dead at fifty-three. Another blonde bombshell of the forties had lost her battle with the bottle, though the official cause was listed as acute hepatitis. Then Susan Hayward was felled by three inoperable brain tumors, though she would hang on for another twenty months. The tragic deaths of three of Hollywood's biggest stars confirmed the old superstition that death comes in threes.

Six hundred mourners attended Betty Grable's funeral at 1:00 P.M. at All Saints Episcopal Church in Beverly Hills, where Betty's former pastor in Las Vegas offered a factual, appropriate eulogy: "Betty Grable was one of the most popular women who ever lived on this earth." The simple closed wooden casket, covered by her favorite flowers, red and white carnations, stood surrounded by a dozen lavish floral pieces. One, a large heart of red carnations from Jessie and Vicki; another, from Harry James.

Harry stood next to Jessie and directly behind Bob Remick during the brief services. Wan and distant, Harry stared straight ahead throughout the funeral, trying to ignore the curious stares of everyone present. One fan who traveled from afar became hysterical when she realized the casket would remain closed. She was removed from the church, screaming, "Open it. *Open* it!" Earlier, another fan, a frail youth, had knelt down before the casket for an entire day.

During the service, Cesar Romero, deeply grieved, nervously tapped his program and shook his head in disbelief. Dorothy Lamour, whose loyalty and love gladdened Betty's last days, was ashen in the stifling July heat, her hands trembling as she signed the guest book. Also present, in addition to scores of "gypsies"—men and women of the choruses—were Alice Faye, Dan Dailey, Mitzi Gaynor, Patsy Kelly, Johnnie Ray, Robert Wagner—and June Haver. Haver's appearance prompted Eve Wynn, Van Johnson's ex-wife, to say to Jeff Parker, "Betty sure would turn over now if she saw *her* here. What in hell is she doing here?"

Betty's favorite song, "On a Clear Day You Can See Forever," was sung by her old friend the owner of the Las Vegas Italian restaurant Battista's. When the service was over, Harry James was the first to depart. Leaving Jessie behind, Harry bolted past a group of celebrities who tried to offer condolences, and exited to a side alley, where he jumped into a waiting car and sped away. Jessie never saw her father again.

Tributes poured in. President Nixon wrote Jessie and Vicki. "Mrs. Nixon and I would like to express our sympathies upon the loss of your mother." Harry James, speaking somewhat impersonally, said, "People who had known her and hadn't seen her in over twenty years came to the funeral. All kinds of people. Grooms from the racetrack. Little people from the studios."

Jackie Coogan said, "I talked to Betty in the hospital about six weeks ago. It [the cancer] had been arrested and I wanted to talk to her about a job. I'd been signed as master of ceremonies for a nostalgic revue on vaudeville to be staged at the Garden State in New Jersey, one of those big theaters that seats seven or eight thousand. It would have been great for me to work with her again. And she'd have loved that too."

"I wanted to marry Betty," George Raft once said, "and would have if I could have gotten free. Once, when she was in New York, Louella Parsons, God rest her soul, ran an item that Betty had been out with Van Johnson. I sent her a telegram signed 'George Van Raft.' Believe me, I carried an awful torch when we came to the end of our road. I used to go into a little bar we liked and have the piano player do 'I Saw You Last Night and Got That Old Feeling.' I didn't see Betty, but when you have loved someone, you always feel close to them."

"A lot of guys aboard ships kept her picture in their lockers," Victor Mature said. "Those kids in the service were all thinking of the gal back home, and she had a beautiful way of bringing back those memories."

Hugh O'Brian, who worked onstage with Betty in *Guys and Dolls,* called her "a great broad."

When reporters approached Darryl Zanuck for a reaction to the death of the most popular star Fox ever developed, he replied, "No comment." A few years later Zanuck would be incapacitated by an inoperable brain tumor that often left him rambling and incoherent. His wife, Virginia, took him back after his ridiculous string of romances with young women. His last days were spent in paranoid seclusion in a well-guarded estate in Palm Springs. After his death in 1979, the Friends of the University of Southern California Libraries tried to get scores of stars to attend a Zanuck tribute, but only a handful showed up.

The most moving eulogy of Betty Grable was expressed in a letter to the editor appearing in the *Los Angeles Times.* Edward Johnson of Palm Desert, California, wrote, "Electing myself to represent about ten million G.I.'s of World War II, I would like to say that Betty Grable instilled in G.I.'s a desire to not only be victorious in that war, but the serene thoughts of the good life back home."

Several days after the burial, Bob Remick and Marjorie drove to Inglewood Memorial Park in the south-central, industrialized section of Los Angeles. In the last few months, the sister and the lover had been bound together in their mutual vigil over Betty. They entered the Sanctuary of Dawn wing where Betty's ashes were interred. A sign over their heads admonished WHISPER PLEASE.

They proceeded down a Gothic marble hall lined with stained-glass windows. Periodically, an automatic timer set off the recorded trills of a hundred canaries, accompanied by organ music.

The walls were filled with crypts. Betty's was marked by a simple bronze plaque—BETTY GRABLE JAMES: 1916–1973, already tarnished. Curiously, Billie's plaque, *above* Betty's, shone brightly. Conn's plaque was at the bottom. Even in death, Billie still ran the show.

# CHAPTER 21

Vicki's husband swooped down on Betty's Las Vegas house, where Bob Remick still lived. Bivens picked and tore through Betty's personal belongings. "This painting must be worth . . ." Bivens calculated, taking the items he wanted, including the silver tea set Samuel Goldwyn had given to Betty as a wedding present when she married Jackie Coogan. Later Marjorie too would descend on Remick. "I want these," Marjorie said, snatching up Betty's shoes, furs, and gowns. She searched in vain for the turquoise-blue gown Betty had worn to the Academy Awards. Bob Remick had hidden it.

"Bob Remick gave up everything to care for Betty and be her companion for eight years," Hollywood columnist Lee Graham wrote. "But there is no mention of him in the will. Bob was always a giver, never a taker. He is glad the money from the sale of the property will go to her two daughters. Jessie can use it. She is separated from her husband, Ronald Yahner, and has two children to support. He loved Betty very much."

Betty's Las Vegas home was auctioned off and sold to the

Tropicana Hotel Corporation to pay the taxes on her estate and satisfy her outstanding debts. Five million dollars in film and stage earnings had been squandered. Remick, fuming, intimated he might bring forth Harry's IOUs still in his possession, but he never did. Remick asked for and received the brown Mercedes. Along with the title to the car, he was given a bill for the outstanding balance on it, which he agreed to pay.

Betty Ritz asked Bob to send her two personal items she was certain no one else would want: Betty's broken black comb, with most of the teeth missing, and her last, chewed-up, nicotine-stained cigarette holder, symbols of their first meeting at the Del Mar racetrack in the 1940s and their last farewell in Las Vegas.

Betty's remaining material possessions, most of which lay in storage, were divided between Jessie and Vicki, as were proceeds from some stock yielding $20,000.

Debbie Reynolds phoned Jessie, asking for all of Grable's costumes for her motion picture museum, a pet project of Debbie's that remains unrealized to this day. Jessie ignored the request, pointing out that Debbie's reputation as a determined star had been too much even for the iron-willed Grable.

Jessie at that time had far more important matters to deal with after the passing of her mother—especially a profound sense of isolation from the family.

"You have to remember," Jessie said, "my sister had her husband and she moved back to him. My aunt moved back to my uncle. I went to nobody but myself and my kids in North Hollywood. I went back there to my empty room and sat there. I had nobody to release my feelings to or to talk to."

Memories of her mother began to haunt Jessie's dreams. "I remember her eyes as [they were] when she died," Jessie said. "Her hands, I remember, stayed normal through her whole ordeal. Real long fingernails, real nice hands. But her eyes changed color to a light blue—like a light behind them. I'd wake up in the middle of the night seeing all that—those eyes. Or she'd be in a coffin and I'd be talking to her and then Bob or someone would come in—and she'd be dead again."

Another recurring dream involved a screaming match between mother and daughter—but whenever Jessie yelled back at her mother, she would be lying there dead.

Betty's beloved costar Dan Dailey, after three unsuccessful marriages and shortly after the suicide of his only son, gave up his will to live. By the time of his death in 1978, Dailey's alcoholism left him unrecognizable and aged beyond his years. The dehydrating, withering effects of liquor also hideously scarred Dailey with the secondary effects of a rare form of skin ulcer.

On March 28, 1980, Betty's old friend and costar Dick Haymes succumbed to the same cancer of the lungs that destroyed Betty's health.

George Raft died from emphysema and leukemia on November 24, 1980. Attorney Sidney Korshak said, "Raft was a man who never hurt or turned his back on anyone."

Marjorie, still wondering what had become of Betty's Oscar gown, died suddenly of a stroke in 1980. Like her mother, Marjorie spent her final years in pain, as the victim of spinal and hip arthritis. Photographer Frank Powolny, who snapped the legendary pin-up picture, died of a heart attack in January 1984 at the age of eighty-four. Though he never became a household name, his great body of photographs—ranging from Janet Gaynor and Shirley Temple to Joan Collins—graced newspapers, magazines, and theater lobbies throughout the world.

It was all downhill for Harry James after Betty died. He rarely mentioned her, and he would not speak to anyone who asked about her. But he often said he would "give his eye teeth" to be able to hit a high C again. He had lost all of his teeth—except one—making it almost impossible for him to anchor his trumpet.

James was a weak man. If anything went wrong on the job or if he had another one of his frequent quarrels with his manipulative manager Pee Wee Monte over money, Harry would return to the bottle and drink twice as much.

His drunkenness became a source of great embarrassment for anyone associated with him. Viewed by some as a drunken gambler, James habitually lost his weekly earnings at the crap tables while simultaneously playing twelve keno cards at a single crack.

Wherever he went Harry carried a trunk filled with bottles of booze. He set it in the wings just offstage. In the middle of a performance, James often walked off and reached into the trunk for a quick double vodka.

Unlike many alcoholics, Harry, while working, was able to gauge just how many drinks he could have before it came time to board the bus for the next gig. He sat in front, near those who did not take drugs, the "squares." The "heads," the drug users, clustered in the back. After ten minutes, Harry always passed out. He would wake up only long enough to help himself to another drink.

In 1979 Frank Sinatra asked Harry to share the spotlight with him at Caesars Palace in Las Vegas for Sinatra's "Fortieth Anniversary in Show Business Show." Sinatra asked James to bring along his lead drummer and piano player, Norm Parker. But when they arrived James was asked to appear only in the opening number, "One O'Clock Jump." Harry, extremely disappointed, complained bitterly of it to Parker. He believed he had been treated in a shoddy manner, and he reminded those close enough to hear that he was the one who had discovered Sinatra in some New Jersey dive forty years before. It so depressed him that he sulked and drank in his dressing room, refusing to attend the fabulous party Sinatra had arranged for "a thousand" of his closest friends. Sadly James didn't live long enough to witness the timelessness of his music as celebrated in the latest Woody Allen film, *Hannah and Her Sisters*, where his recording of "You Made Me Love You" is featured in the music score.

In late 1982, Harry James developed cancer of the lymph nodes and, like Betty, he had to work until two weeks before his death on July 5, 1983—the fortieth anniversary of his marriage to Betty.

Jessie lives today in a small community outside the university town of Eugene, Oregon, a thirty-seven-year-old divorcee and mother of two. "I'm doing what I should have done long ago," she says, referring to her work as an inhalation therapist. She speaks occasionally with Vicki, who now lives with her family in Michigan.

"You know," Jessie says of her sister, "I would never trade places with her. Just because of the many things I've done. She's done a lot of things, too, but I've had experiences she'll never have. She's two *[sic]* years older than I, but from what she's had to deal with, she looks about ten years older—from all the stress she's had."

Throughout the difficult period of sorting out her mother's affairs, Jessie had asked for nothing. Going through Betty's stored furniture, she found a box of photographs. They were of Jessie as an infant. As a child Jessie had begged for some of her baby pictures to be displayed in her mother's bedroom but Betty had denied the existence of any such pictures. And now, here they were.

Later Jessie visited Betty's bank. She found a few documents in the safe-deposit box. At the very bottom lay an envelope containing a note in Betty's hand that read, "Sorry, there's nothing more."